HOMOSEXUALITY IN RENAISSANCE ENGLAND

Between Men ~ Between Woman

Homosexuality in Renaissance England

with a new Afterword

Alan Bray

Columbia University Press
New York

Morningside Edition, with a new afterword and updated bibliography by the author
© 1982 Alan Bray
© 1995 Alan Bray

Library of Congress Cataloging-in-Publication Data
Bray, Alan.
    Homosexuality in Renaissance England / Alan Bray. — 2nd ed.
        p.   cm. — (Between men—between women)
    Originally published: London : Gay Men's Press, 1982.
    Includes bibliographical references (p.   ) and index.
    ISBN 978-0-231-10288-9 (cloth : alk. paper)—ISBN 978-0-231-10289-6
    (pbk. : alk. paper)
        1. Homosexuality, Male—England—History.   2. Homosexuality, Male—
    Social aspects—England.   3. Renaissance—England.   I. Title.
    II. Series.
    HQ76.2.G7B69   1995
    306.76′62′0942—dc20   95–31441
                                                                                CIP
∞
Casebound editions of Columbia University Press books are
printed on permanent and durable acid-free paper.

This edition of my book is dedicated to Graham Wilson, my friend since our childhood together.

Introduction

In 1897 Havelock Ellis's *Sexual Inversion*[1] was published amid uproar and protest. The controversy has long since passed; but in one of many respects the ideas it popularised still exert a powerful influence. Ellis's deliberately sober prose barely disguises a captivating and persuasive picture of the place homosexuality occupied in the Renaissance, and this has acquired an extraordinary currency since the days of the sexual radicals at the turn of the century, of which Ellis was one. Its core is a catalogue of the homosexual poets and painters, philosophers and statesmen of the Renaissance: Michelangelo, Leonardo, Christopher Marlowe, Francis Bacon, these together with a glittering array of Renaissance aristocrats and monarchs and a host of lesser artists are the stuff of which this picture is made. The dark constraints of the monkish Middle Ages were past: sexual and artistic freedom went hand in hand. It is a description which still has scholarly supporters;[2] but more importantly perhaps, it has acquired a popular life of its own and is now likely to represent the expectations many readers will bring to a book dealing with homosexuality in Renaissance England. The reader had better then be warned that these expectations will not be met, that the influential picture of the Renaissance painted by Ellis and the other early apologists for homosexuality is almost entirely a myth. Its slender foundation is an uncritically simple reading of the literature of the time; and it significantly takes no account of the considerable evidence for the deep horror with which homosexuality was widely regarded. It was brilliant propaganda, but it was not sober history. It is the wrong place to begin.

It would though be unfair to Ellis and his circle to suggest that the historical element in their writings was myth and nothing more. What they succeeded in demonstrating, often in the teeth of opposition and at considerable personal cost, was that there was a historical dimension to homosexuality: it had a history. On this basis later historians — the few that were interested to do so — were able to put together a more accurate and critical description.[3] The culmination of this second group of writings is John Boswell's massively scholarly book *Christianity, Social Tolerance and Homosexuality*. This book, which Boswell describes as a history of 'gay people in Western Europe from the beginning of the Christian Era to the fourteenth century', does not go beyond the medieval period. But it is an illuminating opening into the period with which the present book is concerned, in that it includes a description of the growing social intolerance and rigidity that gripped European society in the thirteenth century and fixed the horror of homosexuality, the vice 'not to be named among Christians', which, at the point where this book begins, the Renaissance inherited and perpetuated. The imaginative world of Renaissance England which we are about to enter was set not in a renaissance of antiquity but in the contracting and fearful vision of the close of the Middle Ages.

But the approach of which John Boswell's book is the finest example has a weakness of its own in that it set out to write a history of an essentially unchanging entity, itself above history. This may seem an extraordinary objection. How else could one write a history *of it*? Yet however much a matter of common sense this approach seems to be, at points it appears a blunt tool. And that should make us think again. The eager researcher is first likely to notice a difficulty when considering the terms used for homosexuality in the sources, or rather when trying to pin them down: it soon becomes apparent that this is a search for something that does not exist. Certainly references to homosexuality are easy to find, but one will also find that the terms used carry other meanings as well: the concepts involved are broader. The researcher may then wisely turn to the philosophers or even the theologians of the time in the hope that their more general discussions would be a guide to the way homosexuality is being understood. This is likely to seem safer ground, for it comes as a pleasant surprise to discover alongside them individuals who were not philosophers and theologians saying very similar things, which on the basis of the more careful philosophical expositions can now be clearly understood. The relief should be short-lived, for the researcher will soon begin to notice behaviour which we today would certainly recognise as homosexual but which contemporaries appear to be seeing in altogether other terms. There was an immense disparity in this society between what people said — and apparently believed — about homosexuality and what in truth they did. The evidence for this disparity, at first a nagging doubt, grows to my mind until it is not to be got round. A careful and thorough assembling of comments and reliable facts about homosexuality in Renaissance England, however scholarly, is not of itself sufficient. It is likely to leave one with the feeling that they are the answer to questions which have not yet been asked and as matters stand are not going to be.

The problem is still at root the same: where are we to begin? In 1968 Mary McIntosh published an article in *Social Problems* which was to be a catalyst. Was the contemporary homosexual role, which earlier sociologists and psychologists as well as historians had taken for granted as their starting-point, itself a possible object of study? Was it an appropriate way of framing questions about homosexuality in a different culture or a society of the past? If it was not, and Mary McIntosh argued with passion that this was indeed the case, then historians were free to ask of their material quite new and historically more appropriate questions. It is an approach which has been perceptively developed by Jeffrey Weeks in his studies of homosexuality in late nineteenth- and early twentieth-century English society, combined by him with the allied approaches of symbolic interactionism and more recently of the French historian Michel Foucault.[4] It is broadly in this tradition that the present book is written. It is a history of an aspect of sexuality whose expression has varied radically across different cultures and societies; I have therefore sought to write about homosexuality in the context of a particular historical juncture, largely that of England from the close of the Middle Ages to the middle of the seventeenth century, which for want of a better title may be called Renaissance England.

The book is divided into four chapters, each of which looks at homosexuality from a different viewpoint. The first discharges the historian's primary duty: to see the past in its own terms. Here this means to grasp where homosexuality was placed in the mental universe of the people who lived in that long past society, its place in their world of myth and symbol. The second analyses, now at a distance, its place in the structure of society. There is a striking disparity between these two viewpoints; and the explanation of this is the subject of the third chapter, which is the heart of this book. The fourth chapter looks forward to homosexuality in a later period, that of the late seventeenth and early eighteenth centuries. But this is not put forward as a complete description; my concern is still, indirectly, with the homosexuality of Renaissance England, to show by contrast the transformation history had in store for it.

The explanation for that change is not to be found in any study of homosexuality and society alone, and the conclusion of this book takes it far beyond the questions with which it began. It can scarcely be stressed too strongly or too often that the society of Renaissance England is at an immense distance, in time and culture, from our own; and the great changes which followed it were not only in the social expression of homosexuality but in society itself.

The judgements this book comes to are no more than provisional, tools yet to be tested. This is so for two sharply distinguishable reasons. One lies in that it is only recently that the history of homosexuality has begun to be written in earnest. Certainly it is exhilarating to be with others at the beginning of a new exploration of the past — and the history of homosexuality is exactly that — but by the same token the early narratives of that journey will almost certainly appear partial and incomplete to those who follow on. But this book is also provisional in a further and different sense. From the viewpoint of the academic historian the history of homosexuality is likely to appear as an extension of the history of the family, which started its spectacular career in the mid 1960s with Peter Laslett's *The World We Have Lost;* and this is right in so far as the history of homosexuality draws on the insights of that research, the present book included. But as a matter of simple fact, it was not the history of the family that first gave rise to it. The impetus behind it lay in the growth, in the years since the Second World War, of visible homosexual subcultures in the major cities of the western world, which in the last ten or fifteen years have become increasingly articulate and questioning. And the questions, on the level of the individual or the many, have largely meant asking Who am I? What then are we? I believe historians have something to say to this, for identity without a consciousness in time is impossible; but they should never forget that it was not they to whom it first occurred to ask the questions they are now concerned with and that it is not only in the universities that the answers they give will be put to the test. This book should be judged, firstly, by its capacity to explain the many fragments from the past bearing on homosexuality which are now coming to light, and secondly, by its ability to illuminate the world around us as history has given us it and — this above all else — to play a part in changing it. These are demanding criteria to judge any book by; but in so far as this book fails to meet any of them it should, without hesitation, be put aside.

Chapter One:

Word and Symbol

When the biblical scholars appointed by James I to produce a new version of the Bible (the famous Authorised Version of 1611) came to chapter six of the first Epistle to the Corinthians, they encountered two Greek words which could be associated with homosexuality. Their translation is revealing. The first they translated as 'effeminate', a word which then lacked the specifically homosexual connotations it was later to acquire; the second they translated by a mere description, albeit a description coloured by their disapproval: 'abusers of themselves with mankind'. More than three hundred years later, in the middle of the twentieth century, another panel of scholars considered the same passage and translated it afresh. They would need, they decided, to combine the two Greek words and translate them by a single expression, one of a different order. Both were translated in a word: 'homosexuals'.[1]

What in those three centuries had occurred to bring about such a change? Of course the most obvious explanation is a change in terminology. It was not until the 1890s that the term homosexual first began to be used in English,[2] and none of its predecessors now survive in common speech: ganymede, pathic, cinaedus, catamite, bugger, ingle, sodomite — such words survive if at all in legal forms or deliberate obscenity, or in the classical and theological contexts from which they were drawn. They are creatures of their times. The provenance of the older terms is that amalgam of Christianity and the classical world characteristic of the Renaissance; that of the later term the new psychology of the late nineteenth century.

The term 'homosexual' did not exist in 1611 but (and surely

this is the crucial question) did its equivalent? Only two of the possible candidates, bugger and sodomite, were in general use and neither was synonymous with homosexuality alone. 'Buggery' could be used with as equal ease to mean bestiality as homosexuality. According to the jurist Edward Coke it was a sin committed 'by mankind with mankind or with brute beast or by womankind with brute beast'.[3] 'Sodomy' was a concept as least as broad: 'Sodomitical villanies with men and beasts' was how one writer put it in 1688.[4] It could also be a heterosexual sin. In 1641 the authorities in the Massachusetts Bay colony considered a case of heterosexual relations with under-age girls and, according to Governor Winthrop, 'it was a great question what the kind of this sin was, whether sodomy or rape or etc.'[5] And what are we to make of such a word as 'sodomitess' given in the Authorised Version of the Bible as the alternative translation of 'whore'?[6] Or the names of 'Sodom' and 'Little Sodom' given to the heterosexual brothels of Salisbury Court in Restoration London?[7] Homosexuality was clearly only part of what these words represented.

It is not surprising therefore to find them often closely associated with other sexual sins; the one was all too apt, it was thought, to lead to the other. According to Du Bartas the inhabitants of Sodom and Gomorrah were led on to homosexuality by lesser sins: 'Plenty and pleasure had overwhelmed the while/Sodom and Gomor in all vices vile.' Through rape, adultery and incest they came at last — 'glutted with all granted loves' — to homosexuality.[8] Just such a career was attributed to John Atherton, the bishop of Waterford and Lismore, executed for buggery in 1640. *The Life and Death of John Atherton,* published anonymously shortly after his death, recounts in sensational detail the alleged sexual vices — the same trio of adultery, incest and rape — that in the view of the pamphleteer, culminated in homosexuality and his subsequent execution.[9] These were the same vices that, according to John Wilmot, accompanied the homosexual activity among the bushes of St James's Park in Restoration London:

> And nightly now beneath their shade
> Are buggeries, rapes, and incests made.[10]

Another familiar sequence is John Donne's description of the Court in the 1590s: 'who loves whores, who boys and who

THE SHAMEFVLL ENDE,

Of

Biſhop Atherton,   and his   Proctor Iohn Childe

An illustration from *The Life and Death of John Atherton,* published shortly after Bishop Atherton's execution for buggery in 1640. The figure on the right is John Childe, who was supposed to have been his lover, and who was also executed shortly afterwards.

goats'.[11] In John Marston's *The Scourge of Villanie III* the debauched young man, Luscus, deprived of his mistress consoles himself with his 'Ganymede' and his 'perfumed she-goat'.[12] Jonson's *Sir Volvptvovs Beast* does the same, and then taunts his virtuous wife with his misdeeds:

> Telling the motions of each petticoat
> And how his Ganymede moved and how his goat.[13]

What was the origin of this persistent association of ideas? Clearly, when we come across a writer using the words 'sodomy' or 'buggery' in relation to homosexuality we do the words less than justice if we simply disregard their other meanings. The one word was used because the one concept was intended, and this was a broader concept than simply homosexuality. The notion underlying these passages was not homosexuality but a more general notion: debauchery; and debauchery was a temptation to which all, in principle at least, were subject.

Once this is appreciated several of the apparently very odd remarks made about homosexuality begin to make sense. Debauchery was connected almost as much with the 'plenty and pleasure' that overwhelmed Sodom and Gomorrah as sexual vice and is the context of Edward Coke's conviction that the origin of homosexuality was: 'pride, excess of diet, idleness, and contempt of the poor'.[14] Kings least of all were exempt from the temptation to debauchery, and as staunchly royalist a poet as William Drummond could ask, apparently without embarrassment, that God would keep the King from 'a Ganymede':

> whose whorish breath hath power to lead
> His Majesty such way he list.[15]

When we read George Turbervile's grave explanation that homosexuality was the product of drunkenness ('such filthy sin/ensues a drunken head'),[16] we might at first be inclined to dismiss such an unlikely explanation as a personal oddity — were it not for the fact that the same explanation is given in Richard Middleton's poem *In Eundem*.[17] The oddity is apparent only to us.

To talk of an individual in this period as being or not being 'a homosexual' is an anachronism and ruinously misleading. The temptation to debauchery, from which homosexuality was not clearly distinguished, was accepted as part of the common lot, be it never so abhorred. For the Puritan writer John Rainolds homosexuality was a sin to which 'men's natural corruption and viciousness is prone';[18] when the governor of Plymouth colony, William Bradford, mused in his history of the colony why 'sodomy and buggery (things fearful to name) have broke forth in this land', the first answer he gave was all-embracing: 'our corrupt natures, which are so hardly bridled, subdued, and mortified'.[18a]

This leaves the historian in a quandary. Modern categories may well be misleading but merely adopting those of the period is no real solution: there is no guarantee that they will be used appropriately, which is the essence of the matter. The solution I have adopted is to use the term homosexuality but in as directly physical — and hence culturally neutral — a sense as possible. I have also restricted the scope of the book to questions of male homosexuality. Female homosexuality was rarely linked in popular thought with male homosexuality, if indeed it was recognised at all. Its history is, I believe, best to be understood as part of the developing recognition of a specifically female sexuality.

Whatever solution one adopts, the problem is a salutary warning: the terms in which we now speak of homosexuality cannot readily be translated into those of the sixteenth and seventeenth centuries. There was a breadth in the concepts used that, at the onset, should put us on our guard. We need to carry our preconceptions lightly if we are to see in Renaissance England more than the distorted image of ourselves.

But how much of Renaissance England is really apparent in comments such as these? Poets and playwrights, a humanist scholar, a pamphleteer, a judge, an ambassador and an administrator — how can one generalise from these? Certainly they cast light on the attitudes to homosexuality held among the social groups to which they belonged — or rather group, for if they did not actually belong to the gentry they were attached to it in the way a playwright or a licensed pamphleteer would have had to be — but what of the ninety-five per cent or more of the population who lived below that all-important line dividing gentry from the rest of society, or the finer distinctions between say labourer, yeoman and craftsman? Such groups are more elusive. The records available to the social historian are, by and large, those left by the literate, the educated and the powerful;

and what are they likely to tell us of the many who were none of these things?

It is a problem for which the social historian has always to be on the alert, but it is not an insurmountable one. A poem, a play or a contemporary description is not necessarily circumscribed by the social origins of its author. It can — and usually will — incorporate a host of incidental details inadvertently drawn from society at large, which a careful eye can distinguish: the surprising names, Sodom and Little Sodom, given to the heterosexual brothels of Salisbury Court are preserved in just such a form — in poems by Butler and the Earl of Rochester and a play by John Dryden[19] — but when Dryden's Loveby loudly complains of the two whores who have just so artlessly embarrassed him:

> I am ruined! for ever ruined: plague had you no places in the town to name but *Sodom* and *Luknors-Lane* for lodgings![20]

it is clear that 'Sodom' is no literary artifice but the popular and notorious name for the area. Often the social origins of the authors are not even the major formative element in their work. While Du Bartas's *The Divine Weeks* is clearly an elite production the same can hardly be said of *The Life and Death of John Atherton*, a piece of popular pamphleteering produced at the time when the established social order was losing its grip on the press; the nature of the difference is not in the authors — both were in some degree members of a literate and articulate elite — but in the different audiences for which these works were intended, whose attitudes they reflected and preserved. Quite how popular in the event *The Life and Death of John Atherton* was we do not know, but with some references to homosexuality it is possible to illustrate just how wide was their appeal. One reference of this kind is the description of Sodom and Gomorrah in David Lindsay's *The Monarche*, a classic statement of sixteenth-century attitudes to homosexuality — to which we shall have to return; despite its sophistication the poem had an immense popular appeal, so much so that within a few years of its publication there is evidence that parts of it had been set to popular tunes or were being read aloud in public for the benefit of those who could not read.[21] Nor in this respect was it unique; there survives in the British Library a black letter ballad, to be sung 'to the tune of the nine Muses', published as a broadsheet c. 1570 and entitled *Of the*

Horrible and Woful Destruction of, Sodome and Gomorra.[22]
Works such as these take us far beyond the social origins of their
authors; they are not the voice of the common man or woman,
but what they had to say about homosexuality was something the
village tailor or the London apprentice apparently appreciated,
and so far as their attitudes to homosexuality differed from those
of their masters and betters we can expect them at the very least
to sound a warning note.[23]

If the first major problem is then one of language, the second --
which soon becomes unavoidable — is the other-worldly context
in which references to homosexuality are likely to occur: the poet
Walter Kennedy shows no hesitation in speaking in the same
breath of a sodomite, a werewolf and a basilisk;[24] and sodomites
for Edward Coke were part of an infernal trio of 'sorcerers,
sodomites, and heretics'.[25] The problem of such figures for the
historian is that these are not the stuff of daily life but of myth
and legend, not of experience but of fear.

Nowhere is this more true than in the figure of the Papist,
follower of Antichrist, servant of the terrible King of Spain and,
as the propagandists of the Reformation added, sodomite. The
Popish sodomite is a familiar figure, which takes us into the heart
of the problem, and will be worth looking at at length. Was not
the Papacy itself a 'second Sodom', 'new Sodom',[26] 'Sodom
Fair',[27] nothing but 'a cistern full of sodomy'?[28] With such
propaganda — and it becomes wearisomely familiar — the
Protestant party was doing no more than adapting to its own use
the identification of heresy with sodomy that the Catholic
Church had itself constructed during its confrontation with the
heresies of the twelth century, the identification of religious
deviation with sexual deviation.[29] The celibacy of the Roman
priests could not have fitted it better:

'Lo there is the chastity of the Romish priests,' wrote William
Lithgow, 'who forsooth may not marry and yet may miscarry
themselves in all abominations, especially in sodomy, which is
their continual pleasure and practice.'[30]

Equally amenable to such treatment were the wealthy monastic
orders: 'on whom the vengeance of God is so manifestly declared
for their beastly buggery,' it was confidently asserted after less
elevated parties had done their work, 'that the very places where
they dwelt are not thought worthy to be the dwellings of men but

the caves of brute beasts and venomous worms.'[31] But it was the
Jesuits above all who came to embody in popular mythology the
identification of Popery with homosexuality. Were they not its
open advocates? It was from the Jesuit colleges abroad that
homosexuality was being introduced into England, or so John
Marston claimed,[32] and the author of the encyclopaedic
Heresiography, Ephraim Pagitt, is unlikely to have disagreed:
'their idolatries and sodomitical uncleanness', he noted in his
description of the Jesuits, 'they will defend and maintain.'[33]

The sodomitical Jesuits were not only enemies of true religion:
they were also enemies of the King of England. If they preached
the Papal right to depose a heretical monarch, it was not difficult
to believe that they also preached the lawfulness of rising against a
tyrant. Rebellion against the Church and rebellion against the
State were not concepts easily distinguished in Tudor and Stuart
England, and as might be expected homosexuality played its part
in the folklore of treason as it did in the folklore of Popery; the
one was the natural extension of the other. Buggery, explained
Edward Coke, was treason against the King of Heaven:

> crimen laesae majestatis, a sin horrible, committed against
> the King; and this is either against the King Celestial or
> Terrestial in three manners: by heresy, by buggery, by
> sodomy.[34]

Heresy, homosexuality, and treason are blended in the famous
allegations made against the playwright Christopher Marlowe by
the sinister figure of the informer Richard Baines.[35] For the
authorities the most alarming part would have been the
blasphemous and treasonable nature of the remarks he is
supposed to have made (among others), 'that the first beginning
of religion was only to keep men in awe' and 'that he had as good
right to coin as the Queen of England';[36] but Baines went a step
further and quietly added enough to colour them and enhance
their plausibility. Marlowe, he implies, is a sodomite: 'St John the
Evangelist,' Baines reports Marlowe as saying, 'was bedfellow to
Christ and leaned always in his bosom, that he used him as the
sinners of Sodoma' and 'that all they that love not tobacco and
boys were fools.'[37]

Although a sceptic he is also, according to Baines, a Papist
sympathiser: 'if there be any God or any good religion, then it is in
the Papists.'[38] Such sympathies are what would have been

expected of a traitor and blasphemer and, as Baines was no doubt well aware, added to the plausibility of the whole.[39]

Whether or not there is any truth in Baines's stories, these were connections in which people were inclined to believe: the Papist was a sodomite and a traitor. Yet no one would now be inclined to take such stereotyped propaganda at its face value. It is part of a mythology, embracing werewolves and basilisks, sorcerers and the devilry of the Papists; and it was within its mould that the images of the sodomite were cast. What it leads us into is not the texture of everyday life but the symbolic universe of Elizabethan and Stuart England. It is this that animates them and if we wish to understand what they represented it is where we must begin.

The place homosexuality occupied in that symbolic universe is made clearer by the third of the three figures that Coke linked together. If the heretic and the sodomite were two of the three, the third was the sorcerer.

The association with sorcery, even more than with Popery, is worth looking at closely; it uncovers a crucial element in the relationship homosexuality was thought to have with the universal scheme of things, or rather — as we shall see — was thought to lack.

This is perhaps surprising as there is no sign in the English material that the sexuality of witches was thought to be other than heterosexual, although there was some evidence of this in other parts of Europe. Of course sexual fantasies do appear in English witch lore and there is evidence of the belief that the witch had sexual relations with the Devil or a 'familiar' demon. But this was not homosexuality: if the witch was female the Devil appeared as a man, an incubus, and if the witch was male he appeared as a female, a succubus. The witch's sexual appetite, however inordinate, was none the less heterosexual.[40]

And yet there is a connection: a persistent motif that the child of the witch's diabolical union is a sodomite. 'Hast thou of late embraced some succubus,' the poet John Oldham accused the *Author of a Play called Sodom,* 'And used the lewd familiar for a Muse?'[41] A sodomite, explained the author of *The Times' Whistle,* was 'by some devil got' for 'Such men must be the children of the Devil.'[42] The motif is developed at length in Michael Drayton's poem *The Moone-Calfe,* a fantastic narrative, which opens with a woman representing sinful Earth about to give birth to a child:

> Alas (quoth she) the Devil dressed me thus
> Amidst my riot while that incubus
> Wrought on my weakness; and, by him beguiled,
> He only is the father of the child.[43]

The child is a pair of twins, deformed physically and morally — the mooncalf of the title — whose later vices serve as a convenient peg for Drayton's satiric intentions. Both are sexually debauched: but while the female's debauchery is entirely heterosexual, the male twin keeps both a mistress and 'his smooth-chinned, plump-thighed catamite'.[44] He is a sodomite.

But surprisingly, this was not thought to have been part of the Devil's intention. In *The Moone-Calfe* the Devil is by no means pleased with his child; this 'monstrous birth' is as fearful a thing for him as it is for God; the Devil, in Drayton's mind, had no liking for sodomy:

> Sodom for her great sin that burning sank,
> Which at one draught the pit infernal drank,
> Which that just God on Earth could not abide,
> Hath she so much the devils terrified:
> As from their seat, them well near to exile,
> Hath Hell new spewed her up after this while:
> Is she new risen, and her sin again
> Embraced by beastly and outragious men.[45]

Sodomy, according to *The Life and Death of John Atherton*, is 'more monsterlike than even was devil yet.'[46] In Du Bartas it is a sin:

> Which Hell itself before had never seen,
> A sin so odious that the fame of it
> Will fright the damned in the darksome Pit.[47]

The Devil's reaction to the birth of the mooncalf is no different to the reaction of his servants:

> The Devil if he saw it sure would fear it;
> For by the shape, for aught that I can gather,
> The child is able to afright the father.[48]

What was it about homosexuality that made the Devil fear his own child? Surprisingly, although both Du Bartas and Drayton roundly assert it, neither explain their reasoning. But did they need to? Every culture has a bedrock of shared ideas, sufficiently general as rarely needing to be made explicit; it is this that Du Bartas and Drayton are drawing on. Such ideas tend to elude historians when they are trying to probe the symbolism of a different culture; but when their presence begins to become apparent they are an encouraging sign that the analysis has come close to the heart of that society's symbolic world. It is there that the superficial obscurities are likely to be explained. The explanation of the immediate puzzle of what Du Bartas and Drayton had to say about homosexuality and the Devil lies in the ambiguous position assigned to the Devil in his relationship with God: he was the Great Adversary, but it was an unequal struggle and the outcome was never in doubt; at worst his malice was no more than that of the ape of God, the Simia Dei — his mimic.[49] And what was true of the Devil was also true of the witch, the Devil's counterfeit of the saint. As the saint strove for union with God and was permitted to express that longing in the language of heterosexual love, so — it was thought — the witch's union with the Devil was a hideous material parody of that ideal love. The Church had constructed its demonology in its own image, and although homosexuality might be the product of the Devil's union with the witch, this product was unforeseen. Homosexuality had no place in the Kingdom of Hell because it had none in the Kingdom of Heaven.

What then was homosexuality if it was of neither Heaven nor Hell? It was unmistakably related to the myth, but only indirectly: the myth insists in fierce terms on what homosexuality is not but does not say what it is. However it coexisted with a parallel myth equally influential, which is more revealing. If this unequal struggle — the story of the Fall and Redemption — was the myth of God the Redeemer, its complement was the myth of God the Creator. At first sight this seems even less helpful than the other, for whatever homosexuality was clearly it was not God's creation; yet on close analysis, this myth can be seen to define what homosexuality is by the very completeness with which it excludes it.

Above all else, what God created was order. Nature, according to Thomas Browne, was the 'universal and public manuscript' of God.[50] 'All things began in order,' he writes, 'so shall they end, and so shall they begin again; according to the ordainer of order and mystical mathematics of the City of Heaven.'[51] The mystical

mathematics of the City of Heaven was the image of an
underlying unity in creation that, more than any other, had such a
fascination for Thomas Browne. But it was only one of many. The
chain of 'degree' that linked all living creatures, from the
humblest to the most exalted angels, expressed the same idea
(Thomas Browne's 'ladder and scale of creatures'[52]), as did the
harmonies of music or the unity in diversity of a courtly or a folk
dance:

> Mystical dance, which yonder starry sphere
> Of planets and of fixed in all her wheels
> Resembles nearest, mazes intricate,
> Eccentric, intervolved, yet regular
> Then most, when most irregular they seem;
> And in their motions harmony divine
> So smooths her charming tones that God's own ear
> Listens delighted.[53]

If order and 'degree' were the rule in the created universe at large,
would not the same also be true in individual and social life?
Without them:

> Strength should be the lord of imbecility,
> And the rude son should strike his father dead.

And Shakespeare also wrote:

> When beggars die there are no comets seen;
> The heavens themselves blaze forth the death of princes.[54]

It is a view of the world in which Nature is a unity, as is its
Creator: 'And therefore, being the Rule, He cannot be
irregular.'[55] 'So that,' as Sir John Fortescue wrote, 'there is
nothing which the bond of order does not embrace.'[56]

Nothing except an inescapable possibility: that the chaos of the
first day of Creation when 'the earth was without form, and
void'[57] might come again. It is here that homosexuality had its
place in the myth, altogether outside the ordered world of
Creation. In Michael Drayton's *Peirs Gaveston* the Creation
retreats in horror when Gaveston's love for Edward II falls into
homosexuality:

> The Heavens to see my fall doth knit her brows,
> The vaulty ground under my burden groaneth,
> Unto mine eyes, the air no light allows,
> The very wind my wickedness bemoaneth.[58]

It is the context in which George Turbervile, when he visited Moscow as Elizabeth I's ambassador, sets his description of the homosexuality he encountered in Russian society; it is the product, he writes back to England, of 'a savage soil, where laws do bear no sway', and twice he tells the reader that this is a land where 'lust is law'.[59] The principle of law, as Richard Hooker explained it in his *Of The Laws of Ecclesiastical Polity*, represented more than legislation; it was the principle of order behind the apparent multiplicity of creation:

> That which doth assign unto each thing the kind, that which doth moderate the force and power, that which doth appoint the form and measure of working, the same we term a *Law*.[60]

> See we not plainly that obedience of creatures unto the law of nature is the stay of the whole world?[61]

Homosexuality was not part of Hooker's law of nature. It was not part of the chain of being, or the harmony of the created world or its universal dance. It was not part of the Kingdom of Heaven or its counterpart in the Kingdom of Hell (although that could unwittingly release it). It was none of these things because it was not conceived of as part of the created order at all; it was part of its dissolution. And as such it was not a sexuality in its own right, but existed as a potential for confusion and disorder in one undivided sexuality. Hence the absence already commented on of any satisfactory parallel for the contemporary use of 'homosexuality' in the sense of an alternative sexuality. What sodomy and buggery represented — and homosexuality was only part of these — was rather the disorder in sexual relations that, in principle at least, could break out anywhere. It is this frame of mind we have already encountered in Governor Bradford's reflections on why 'sodomy and buggery (things fearful to name) have broke forth in this land oftener than once':

> It may be in this case as it is with waters when their streams are stopped or dammed up: when they get passage they flow with more violence and make more noise and disturbance, than when they are suffered to run quietly in their own channels. So wickedness being here more stopped by strict laws and the same more nearly looked unto, so as it cannot run in a common road of liberty as it

would and is inclined, it searches everywhere and at last
breaks out where it gets vent.[62]

At last it breaks out — the same assumption and the same
symbolism appear in David Lindsay's description of homosexuality in the antediluvian world, which he held responsible for
the Universal Deluge, its counterpart in the world of Nature.[63] It
was also the rationale of the claim that the celibacy of Roman
priests was the cause of their alleged homosexual sins: the
bulwark against sexual debauchery, in the minds of the
Protestant reformers, was marriage; that gone and all manner of
sodomy and buggery would break forth.

Such a mental universe is alien to us now. In John Taylor's
narrative of the reign of Edward II in his *The English Monarchs*, it
is not the homosexual nature of the King's passion for Gaveston
— a subject on which Taylor is ambiguous — that brings him to
disaster; that would not be an unfamiliar idea. In Taylor's history
the catastrophe is brought about by Edward's offence against
order, his 'immoderate love'.[64] It is of a class with the lovers in the
whirlwind in Dante's *Inferno*, whose disordered love is given
symbolic form in the wildness of the storm on which they are
carried.[65] A conscious act of the imagination is needed if we are to
grasp what is intended when homosexuality is described as a
'wild' thing in a sodomy trial in sixteenth-century Edinburgh;[66] or
when an anonymous clerk in the Middlesex Sessions of the Peace
carefully records that the sodomy of which a Hoxton yeoman was
accused is 'contra naturalem ordinem';[67] or when the far more
illustrious Edward Coke warned that a valid indictment for
buggery must describe the crime as 'contra ordinationem
Creatoris et naturae ordinem'.[68] To those who wrote them — and
presumably to those who first read them — there was nothing
vague or imprecise in these descriptions, far more so than we will
appreciate if we do not read them in the cultural context in which
they were written; their edge is given by an ordered conception of
existence in relation to which homosexuality was defined — or
rather from which it was excluded — as part of a universal
potential for disorder which lay alongside an equally universal
order. It was part, in a word, of its shadow.

How did these images of homosexuality come to hold such a
grip on the imagination of our ancestors? The detached
twentieth-century observer is inclined to suspect that a need was

being satisfied; and the suspicion is only strengthened by what we know of the sodomite's two legendary companions, the Papist and the witch. Each fulfilled, in one respect at least, a similar function: they were explanations for misfortune.

In his *Religion and the Decline of Magic* Keith Thomas describes how accusations of witchcraft

> served as a means of accounting for the otherwise inexplicable misfortunes of daily life. Unexpected disaster — the sudden death of a child, the loss of a cow, the failure of some routine household task — all could, in default of any more obvious explanation, be attributed to the influence of some malevolent neighbour.[69]

An accusation of witchcraft was no doubt a convenient means of avoiding responsibility or saving face, but at other times it seems a more genuinely puzzled response of someone at a loss to explain the hardship being suffered. And unlike the orthodox explanation — that the adversity was the will of God — it provided a course of action.

But not all misfortune can plausibly be attributed to the witchcraft of a malevolent neighbour, and this is particularly so of the troubles and disasters encompassing whole communities. A more credible explanation for misfortune on this scale was that a national enemy was at work; and in the Papists one was ready to hand, for the Papists were not the remnants of pre-Reformation Catholicism — that had effectively disappeared with the Reformation — but, whether converts or not, they were the adherents of an active mission and — what is more to the point — one directed from abroad.[70] The suspicions this gave rise to were more than those of treasonable plotting (although the Jesuits in particular were regularly accused of that). The stories of Papist villany, fanciful though they may seem, were widely believed, and the Papists were variously accused of bringing the plague, burning towns, even of infiltrating Parliament disguised as Puritans and — for their own black-hearted ends — instigating the Civil War.[71]

But there was a type of human suffering, inseparable from the vulnerability of the human condition itself, that even a fifth column within the gates could not credibly be held responsible for: the scourges of natural disaster — of disease, of epidemic and flood — ills attributable only to an act of God, no mere formula in a pre-scientific age. But the Hand of God was not a sufficient explanation likely to satisfy either those who were suffering or the troubled religious believer; the Hand of God it might have to be, but another element was needed if the explanation was to make sense.

And in homosexuality one was found. There is one inescapable part of its mythology that illustrates this. Of all the many images of homosexuality the English Renaissance affords, one above all recurs over and over again: the catastrophe that overwhelmed the cities of Sodom and Gomorrah at the hands of an angry God. Even when not the ostensible subject, it seems never to be far from the mind of the writer when homosexuality is mentioned. It is not an obvious feature in Coke's *Institutes*, but as the biblical references in the margin make clear it forms the background to the section on buggery and the justification — for that is what the section amounts to — for its punishment.[72] It was the origin of one of the two terms most commonly used for homosexuality and was what came most readily to hand when a round-about description was needed of the vice not to be named among Christians.[73] No one who brings together a large number of references to homosexuality from sixteenth- (and seventeenth-) century England can fail to be impressed by the number of times this one biblical reference recurs. But what is most striking and significant is not merely the number of times the story appears but the variety and originality shown in its retelling, characteristics one does not usually associate with Renaissance literature — the period of the emblem books, of *Pilgrim's Progress* and the self-conscious imagery of the Metaphysical poets. Yet the story is to be seen adapted with equal ease for the purpose of religious controversy as in a popular ballad, the writings of a humanist scholar or a piece of social satire. The outrageous obscenities of Christopher Fishbourne's Restoration drama *Sodom or the Quintessence of Debauchery* are an illustration of how far this could be taken.[74] The surprising flexibility of the story is an indication of how much weight we need to give it as a piece of popular mythology. It is only when conventional imagery is close to contemporary attitudes that it is possible to adapt it with much freedom; and the highly formal symbols of the Renaissance frequently betray a weakening of confidence, in them and in the attitudes they presuppose.[75] Against this background the treatment of the story of Sodom and Gomorrah stands out sharply; its vitality reveals just how close it was to contemporary ideas. What then is it saying? In all its many forms one element of the story continually reappears: the miserable end of Sodom and Gomorrah — perhaps by plague, perhaps in an earthquake or by fire, but certainly in an overwhelming upheaval in nature.

Just such catastrophic associations are skilfully, and revealingly, used in David Lindsay's poem *The Monarche*.[76] Ostensibly the poem is a history of the world: in reality it is a thinly disguised anti-Papal tract exposing the Pope as Antichrist, in which the consequences of homosexuality play a subtle structural role. The ground is prepared early on in the descriptions of the Deluge and of Sodom and Gomorrah: in each, as Lindsay tells the story, it was homosexuality which brought down God's anger in the form of these immense upheavals in nature, and the reader at this stage was likely to be content to accept the poem's explanation. But then we come to Papal Rome — that 'cistern full of sodomy' — and the trap is sprung: if the Pope has tolerated sodomy among his priests, the reader is expected to know what is to happen next, as indeed it does in Antichrist's downfall at the hands of an avenging God. His fate, within the logic of the poem, was implicit already in the natural disasters that overwhelmed Sodom and Gomorrah, and also Noah's world, so long ago.

It was because of the catastrophe and suffering sodomy was thought to bring in its train that it was the 'masculine misery' — the phrase is William Lithgow's[77] — and this idea was at the heart of the hostility homosexuality aroused. When the Earl of Castlehaven was tried in 1631 for rape and sodomy the Attorney General, Sir Robert Heath, warned that his crimes were: 'of that pestiferous and pestilential nature that if they be not punished will draw from Heaven heavy judgements upon this kingdom.' By the end of the trial he is no longer talking of these judgements of God merely as a possibility; they were already there.

> By these abominations the land is defiled; and therefore the Lord doth visit this land for the iniquity thereof.

> That God may remove and take away from us His plagues, let this wicked man be taken away from amongst us.[78]

His knowledge of these plagues was derived from something more reliable than fallible report; he had the assurance that comes from knowing that something exists because it must do. And as much as the stories of Sodom and Gomorrah, his concern was with that part of human suffering that cannot be directly attributed to any individual or group of individuals; it was God's doing and His righteous anger.

But in holding the horrors of homosexuality responsible for the divine wrath a number of needs were satisfied together, for homosexuality as we have seen was not part of the created order; rather it was part of its dissolution. In projecting onto homosexuality the cause of this fundamental malaise and thus placing the cause outside the created order altogether, not only had an explanation for the malaise been found, but one that did not undermine the concept of a single divinely-ordained universal order. Indeed it strengthened it and — for this was no mere abstraction — in doing so strengthened the established social order that claimed to be its reflection in the world. It was a disarmingly simple answer operating within a complex system of ideas: it was the fault of the sodomites.

But the Attorney General did not say it was the fault of the sodomites. He said it was the fault of the Earl of Castlehaven, and we might perhaps be forgiven were we to dismiss his remarks as the ravings of a madman. We would be hard put however to find any contemporary support for this; in fact quite the reverse. The contemporary pamphleteer of the Earl's trial quotes the Attorney General's speech with obvious respect; it was not nonsense to him.[79]

There is also a second, equally puzzling, element: why, in any case, should the whole of society suffer through the activities of a minority of obdurate sodomites, or indeed, if the Attorney General is to be believed, through the actions of a single individual? The idea may now seem strange, but did it then? In a broader form it is an idea one soon becomes familiar with in the English Renaissance, when Thomas Browne could write that it was more than 'a pleasant trope of rhetoric' to call ourselves 'a microcosm, or little world':

> There is all Africa and her prodigies in us; we are that bold and adventurous piece of Nature which he that studies wisely learns in a compendium what others labour at in a divided piece and endless volume... There is no man alone, because every man is a microcosm and carries the whole world about him.[80]

It is the corollary of the belief in a single universal order, not atomised but wholly present in each individual part so that the actions of one individual could have repercussions throughout the whole. And if those could bring about a universal disaster? There was a simple and obvious remedy: 'let this wicked man be taken away from amongst us.'

We have come across this before. It is apparent early on that there is no clear line to be drawn between contemporary attitudes to homosexuality and to debauchery as a whole. As such it was a temptation to which all, in principle at least, were subject: a vice to which 'men's natural corruption and viciousness is prone.'[81] Yet more was involved in this than the nature of debauchery. Its logic is the microcosm: if it was a potential in the universe at large so it was, however feared, in each individual human heart.

Were we now to sit down with John Rainolds among his books in Elizabethan Oxford, or indeed with the unknown writer who set the story of Sodom and Gomorrah to a popular tune, or with William Bradford in far-distant New England, and ask them: 'How can it be that sodomy is in all our natures and yet so monstrous a thing that the actions of one sodomite can bring untold misery on humankind at the hands of an angry God?' — they would probably be unable to answer the question. They would be unlikely to grasp that there was any problem that needed an explanation. And if we do not hear them say this — as indeed we may not, armed with the prejudices of a remote time as to what is to be taken seriously and what dismissed as mere rhetoric — then it is because we do not listen. If we do listen but do not believe that this is the real reason for their hostility to homosexuality — and this is more forgiveable — we should not, though, forget that their conception of reality differed in many ways from our own. When the Attorney General conjured up plagues we cannot even now see, and raved that all would be well if only 'this wicked man' was done away with, he was merely expressing, with precision and a clarity rarely considered necessary, the commonly held assumptions as to the nature of homosexuality characteristic of his society and time.

Randolph Trumbach has perceptively written that:

> ... we ought to study the historical forms of sexual behaviour not simply because they are interesting in themselves, but rather because sexual behaviour (perhaps more than religion) is the most highly symbolic activity of

any society. To penetrate to the symbolic system implicit in any society's sexual behaviour is therefore to come closest to the heart of its uniqueness.[82]

The starting point for such a study is a society's own understanding of sexuality; yet the result is quite likely to take us beyond sexuality altogether — and with Renaissance England it is unavoidable — into the broad scope of its symbolic universe, far removed from the texture of everyday life. But does it have to end there? Is it possible to go beyond the mythology of demons and witches, of microcosm and macrocosm, to the place homosexuality quietly occupied in the daily lives of labourers, artisans, merchants and gentry? Yes, I believe it is, and to that task we must now turn.

Chapter Two:

The Social Setting

On the 4th of June 1599 the agents of the Bishop of London made a bonfire at Stationers' Hall. Its fuel was the books they had been collecting over the previous three days, since the banning of those troublesome 'satires or epigrams' which the Bishop of London was determined to be rid of once and for all, suspecting them (with reason) of a too lively interest in the very vices they claimed to be censuring. Marston's *Scourge of Villanie*, Guilpin's *Skialetheia*, Middleton's *Micro-Cynicon* — these and others like them had apparently come to the end of their notorious careers. But in the long run, as is often the case, a bonfire proved an ineffective form of censorship; the books survived, and after a decent interval — but now rather more circumspectly — others of the same kind began again to appear.[1] For the study of homosexuality in the English Renaissance it was a happy outcome, because among the vices and follies of the time they purported to be exposing homosexuality made a frequent and graphic appearance:

Behold at length in London streets he shows...
His clothes perfumed, his fusty mouth is aired.
His chin new swept, his very cheeks are glazed.
But ho, what Ganymede is that doth grace
The gallant's heels, one who for two days' space
Is closely hired?[2]

And when himself he of his home can free,
He to the city comes, where then if he
And the familiar butterfly his page
Can pass the street, the ordinary and stage
It is enough and he himself thinks then

To be the only, absolutest of men...
Doublet and cloke with plush and velvet lined,
Only his headpiece that is filled with wind.
Rags, running horses, dogs, drabs, drink and dice
The only things that he doth hold in price.
Yet, more than these, naught doth him so delight
As doth his smooth-chinned, plump-thighed catamite.[3]

Descriptions similar to these two, which are by John Marston and Michael Drayton, can be found in the satires of Ben Jonson or Edward Guilpin, Richard Brathwaite, John Donne or Thomas Middleton.[4] On this point they are remarkably consistent: the sodomite is a young man-about-town, with his mistress on one arm and his 'catamite' on the other; he is indolent, extravagant and debauched.

Have we then so easily found what we are looking for, an eye-witness account of how homosexuality appeared in the society of Elizabethan and Jacobean London? The answer is a clear and unequivocal no. One obvious objection is that these are stock figures not identifiable individuals. Of the objections which could be made this is actually the least telling. Against it must be set the unavoidable problems involved in writing social history on the basis of such 'identifiable individuals'. How does the historian go about drawing general conclusions from them? Are they likely to be representative at all? These, at least, are descriptions of sexual life that their authors claimed had a general significance. And they resemble each other too much to be merely their own creations; in one sense they are communal products. The problem is rather that when one looks closely at them it becomes apparent just how little they are the stuff of social life and how much the product of purely political or literary influences. The word 'satire' raised certain precise — and distinctly uncouth — expectations. It was expected that a satirist would take a coarse delight in exposing obscenity and grossness. He was no detached observer; it was assumed that he would exaggerate and rail at his readers. In such circumstances, extravagant descriptions of sexual debauchery are not now likely to carry much weight. Nor is this the only literary convention which on close examination can be detected in these descriptions. The portrayal of wealth and dissipation — and specifically of luxurious clothing and the use of cosmetics — as symptomatic of sexual vice draws on a well-established tradition; Renaissance satire as a whole makes the same assumption, as indeed did the medieval 'complaint' that preceded it.[5] A third literary influence, arguably the most pervasive of all, is that of Juvenal. All these writers would have acknowledged the classical satires of Juvenal as the model of what satire ought to be; without necessarily plagiarising him, his themes and his manner were something they were all conscious of and in some degree influenced by. And one of these themes was homosexuality. It leaves us with a problem; in trying to evaluate their own references to homosexuality, the danger is that what we are seeing is not Renaissance London but second-century Rome at one remove.

The satirists' portrayal of homosexuality in terms of sexual licence can, then, be amply accounted for by their literary background; it is not a convincing source for social history. But what of their related but more specific claim that homosexuality was the vice of the gentry? If true it would obviously be of the first importance as a piece of social observation. But before coming to a conclusion about this there are two reservations that should be born in mind. Firstly, although there is on this point remarkable consistency among these writers, it is not complete: on some occasions, when it suited their purposes, they are willing to claim precisely the opposite. An instance of this is Philip Stubbes's remarks on homosexuality in the Elizabethan theatre. The theatre of this time was frequented by virtually all social groups, and when — with a Puritan's distaste for drama — he set out to malign it with a charge of encouraging sodomy he had to accommodate this fact. Stubbes's description, then, necessarily weighs in against the whole audience, and not merely the gentry. When the play is over, Stubbes writes:

> these goodly pageants being ended, every mate sorts to his mate, everyone brings another homeward of their way very friendly, and in their secret conclaves covertly they play the Sodomites or worse.[6]

Another author who, to suit his own purpose, did not claim that homosexuality was peculiarly the vice of the gentry was the author of *The Times' Whistle*, who was at pains to prove that homosexuality was something 'the whole land is thus plagued with' without singling out any one group.[7] In this respect Philip Stubbes and the author of *The Times' Whistle* had intentions different from those of the satirists as a whole; and when they assembled their material they at the very least arranged it to suit their purposes. It leaves one wondering whether the other satirists were likely to have been any more objective.

The second point is that it is not the gentry as such but specifically the London gentry who are being disparaged. At first sight at least, it does seem plausible that there would have been more opportunities for homosexual contact in a large and complex city such as London, whatever conclusions one comes to on the question of which social groups were involved. It is also a conclusion some twentieth-century historians have arrived at by analogy with our own times: it is in the more tolerant environment of the inner cities that homosexuality has become a widely available alternative; could not the same have been true of seventeenth-century London?[8] Certainly London was already a great city in the Elizabethan period: by 1580 its population had reached 123,000, and was to rise to half a million over the following century.[9] But the analogy, although plausible, is misleading. London was not a world apart. Firstly it depended on a flow of immigrants from the countryside, who continued to be influenced by the way of life they had so recently left; and the inward flow was matched by an outward flow in the periodic exodus in search of work, particularly at harvest time when large numbers regularly left the city to work in the surrounding countryside.[10] The result is that at any point in this period many of London's inhabitants would only a short time before have been living in rural areas or smaller towns and quite likely would soon be doing so again. Nor was the situation different for the London gentry who, although they might be attached to London by an office at Court, would usually have their roots in a country estate.

In such circumstances it would be unwise to assume that sexual life was less subject to traditional moral codes in London than it was outside it. And indeed there is evidence to the contrary. The proportion of illegitimate births in the London parish registers of the period is no higher than in the contemporary registers of parishes outside London, and the same is probably true of the number of suicides.[11] In those respects the traditional moral codes retained their influence despite London's rapid urbanisation. It should not therefore come as a surprise that accusations of sodomy which appear in the rolls of the Middlesex Sessions of the Peace (the Quarter Sessions responsible for London outside the City itself) are not noticeably different from those in similar records outside London; certainly there is no sign whatsoever of the figure to be met with so frequently in the pages of the satirists.[12]

But if there is no reason to think that homosexuality played any greater part in sexual life in London than it did elsewhere, why then did these writers — and with such consistency — claim otherwise? The explanation is in their attitude to London itself — or rather to one part of it: the Court at Westminster and the army of dependents it attracted. It was a political antagonism, the indignation of the 'Country' party, the opposition to the Court and all its works that was to have its triumph at the calling of the Long Parliament. It drew on the resentment of the gentry — in their own eyes the natural rulers of the counties — who were excluded from the golden circle of lucrative Court appointments provided, or so they believed, at their own considerable expense.[13] It was the Court — the extravagant, overblown, parasitic Renaissance Court — not homosexuality which was the focus of their attention. What homosexuality provided was a powerfully damaging charge to lay against it; at what should have been the stronghold of the kingdom there was only weakness, confusion and disorder. What could have fitted better?[14]

Is there anything left? When all the purely literary and political elements in these writings have been discounted, we might be left wondering whether they are of any use at all as pieces of social observation. The answer surprisingly is still yes, for despite all their bias and self-conscious artistry they were satires and not works of fiction; they were intended to hurt, and without a basis in reality they would have lost their edge. But where these writings are of most use as social description is in those aspects where their writers were least engaged: in the incidental details, which have little immediate bearing on what they were about and which they had least reason or desire to adapt to their purposes.[15] The procedure I have adopted is to disregard those elements in descriptions of homosexuality that can be attributed to literary influence or political bias; it is sometimes possible to return to them at a later stage when they are supported by other evidence, but as a working rule I have eliminated them in the first instance. As a result we are left with a collection of incidental comments about homosexuality, often tiny fragments but not a mere miscellany. This result is surprisingly coherent; these minor details are strikingly consistent both among themselves and in relation to what we know of homosexuality in the period from other sources. And it is also possible to discern in them some of the distinctive characteristics of English society from the close of the Middle Ages to the last decades of the seventeenth century. If we are willing to sift it out, what we are looking for is there.

But this is not a task that can be attempted in isolation. Valuable sources though I believe these satires to be, they are most convincing when supported by other evidence unconnected with them; and we may come across this almost anywhere, in poetry and drama, in pamphlets and popular ballads, in the casual remarks of historians and theologians of the time, even in travel books; there are virtually no limits to the area where references to homosexuality are likely to crop up. But the source most likely to be turned to is in some ways the most difficult to interpret, the prosecutions for sodomy and buggery that appear in the surviving court records. Inevitably a good deal of time will be taken up with these valuable but easily misleading sources; and, before returning to the satirists to draw out some of the conclusions to be found there, we shall need to take a critical look at the way homosexuality appeared in these records, if we are to avoid the pitfalls they hold for the unwary researcher.

Why are court records so difficult to interpret? Certainly they appear to be a sober and objective record of the incidents that brought the individual before the courts, of the accused's name and frequently also of where he or she lived and the accused's occupation. After the obvious bias and downright distortions of a John Marston or a Thomas Middleton one is likely to turn to them with relief. However the relief will be short-lived, or ought to be, for they bring with them a host of problems.

Anyone who begins work for the first time on the indictments in the Assize records — probably the most approachable and succinct of all the judicial records — has before him or her that unpleasant moment, usually brought on by reading J.S. Cockburn's famous article in the *Journal of the Society of Archivists*,[16] when it becomes apparent that these documents are in large part no more than convenient legal fictions. The clerk who prepared them was concerned above all to see that they should be in the correct legal form: if they were not the indictment could fall on a technicality. But the huge increase in the number of cases to be heard in the late sixteenth century and the widespread failure of Justices of the Peace to act as prosecutors made it increasingly difficult for him to achieve this. The result was that the clerk made do as best he could, completing the indictment with a stock phrase or an invention tailored to fit the facts. The government apparently knew of the practice — apparently even expected and approved of it — and behind its façade the judge meted out a rough justice. The conclusion of Professor Cockburn — the foremost expert on the Assizes — was that no less than 'a majority of assize indictments, while technically satisfying the legal requirements, are factually worthless.' [17]

It is a serious problem — the first of several — but there are ways of minimising it. Professor Cockburn has himself drawn attention to the greater reliability of recognizances, bonds binding a named individual to appear to stand trial or to give evidence: for the local supervision to be at all effective, they obviously needed a greater degree of accuracy than the indictments. For similar reasons the Quarter Sessions papers, those of the local Justices of the Peace (who from 1563 were empowered to hear cases of buggery), are also likely to be more reliable than the Assize indictments. Moreover the Quarter Sessions papers may well refer to the same individual on a number of occasions, and the details recorded can be checked against each other. Also some of the more notorious cases produced contemporary pamphlet literature, which can be as good as or even better than the official records.

We need then to distinguish between those records which are likely to be reliable guides and those which are not; but is it in fact clear what they are guides to? The question is not as simple as it might appear. The primary purpose of court rolls and registers was to provide a record of the court's own procedure, i.e. a record of what the accused was supposed to have done and the action taken in the courts, which is not necessarily a record of what actually had occurred. The Gaol Delivery Register of the Middlesex Sessions of the Peace for 1613[18] contains the following terse entry: 'Albanus Cooke for buggery with John Townsend.' The corresponding indictment in the Sessions Rolls adds a little more: John Townsend, it tells us, was an adolescent and Alban Cooke was also charged with assaulting him.[19] But did he? The problem is not with the records themselves, as the Middlesex Sessions records are largely reliable; there is no reason to doubt that Alban Cooke was indicted as the record shows, but it also

notes that he pleaded not guilty and was acquitted. What then
are we to make of it? It is no real solution to rely on whether or
not someone accused of sodomy is found guilty: the verdict may
have been wrong; he may have been convicted on only part of the
evidence, or indeed acquitted on a technicality. And in many
cases we do not even know what the verdict was. How then can
we ever know with any reasonable certainty what had actually
happened?

There is an additional difficulty for the researcher in that only
a fraction of the notes made during the court proceedings have
survived. There are gaps covering several years in virtually all the
collections; and some of the most revealing documents, such as
depositions, were never intended to be permanently preserved.
Even where a series appears to be complete over a given period,
we should always be alive to the possibility — which can on
occasion be demonstrated — that individual cases have
disappeared or were never recorded. The result is that, with a few
exceptions, any statistical analysis is out of the question.

Court records are fragmentary in another sense also. It was
the clerk's task to make a record that satisfied the requirements
of the legal process: he was not concerned to make a full record of
the facts of the kind we would like to see. The result is that the
notes he did make are stark, brief, conventional and unrevealing.
What are we to make of the following intriguing but baffling
entry in the Order Book of the Western Assizes dated 11 March
1647?

> Whereas Domingo Cassedon Drago a negro is to be
> removed by His Majesty's writ of habeas corpus out of
> the gaol of this county and is to be sent into the county of
> Essex, to be tried there at the next Assizes for a buggery
> by him committed; and whereas there is a poor boy named
> William Wraxall now remaining in the custody of Edward
> Graunte tithingman of Northwood, which is to be sent to
> the said Assizes for evidence against the said negro to
> prove the said fact; it is therefore thought fit and ordered
> by this court that the said boy shall be forthwith delivered
> over to the Sheriff of this county, who is desired to take
> such care that the said boy may be sent to the said Assizes
> with the said negro by some honest man who will be
> careful to produce the said boy at the trial of the said
> negro to prove the said fact.[20]

Who were these people? What had brought them here? Judging by his name, Domingo Cassedon Drago had come to England from one of the Spanish colonies, which raises more questions than it solves. And the 'poor boy' William Wraxall — how had he become separated from his parents, as appears to have been the case? How had they met? Was this a casual encounter that had gone disastrously wrong and landed Drago in court, or had they known each other for some time? There is no way we can answer these questions or others like them. We do not even know what happened to them in Essex, assuming that they were indeed sent there, as there is no reference to either of them in the Essex Assize files as they now stand.[21] The lives of these two humble people who lived so long ago are brilliantly illuminated for us for only a moment and then — nothing. It is intensely frustrating.

There is also perhaps something else about this document to unsettle us: of all the figures we might expect to see in seventeenth-century England, is it not surprising that the prisoner in the county gaol should have been black? A black face would have been an unusual sight indeed in England in 1647; did that, one might well wonder, have something to do with why Drago found himself in court? It is a question we shall return to, but it raises a more general point about the use of court records in writing sexual history that we shall need to consider here; is the impression they give at first sight misleading, of revealing the intimate sexual behaviour of the many ordinary men and women who appear in them? What determined what would appear before the courts and the details thought worth recording? Perhaps one should say rather who determined this, as such matters were for the courts themselves to decide. What we are seeing are the concerns and the attitudes of a social elite. Certainly legal records tell us a great deal about the workings of the courts in relation to the regulation of sexual behaviour, but are they a reliable guide to anything else? It would be a rash historian who lightly swept aside that question.[22]

Court records are a far more limited source for the history of homosexuality than they are likely to appear at first sight. Fragmentary, one-sided and a record of fact only in a very limited sense, they are always difficult to interpret; and they are often dangerously inaccurate. But even at their best all they can be expected to reveal is the sexual activity which brought the individuals into court. They have little or nothing to say about their motives; they do not tell us how the figures involved saw themselves or the meanings they or others attached to their actions. And what use is a history of sexuality that goes no further than that? A history of homosexuality based wholly, or even largely, on such material would be at best a poor, soulless thing and at worst a travesty of the truth.

The solution to the problem lies in integrating this material into something that is likely to give a more realistic perspective. This can be partly achieved by combining it with contemporary literary descriptions of homosexuality, which although they have their own problems compensate for the unavoidable limitations inherent in court records. But alone this is not enough. It is also partly a matter of method. The kinds of questions we ask — and this is equally true of literary material as of legal records — need to be posed in a sufficiently broad setting. We need to read these documents, firstly, in the light of the prejudices, the myths and the common symbolism of the society to which their authors belonged; and, secondly, they need to be placed in the contexts and forms of its social life. The first was the concern of the last chapter, the second that of the present.

We must begin with the land. The economy of England in the sixteenth and seventeenth centuries was overwhelmingly rural, to an extent which is difficult for someone living in Europe or North America today to visualise. It was the land itself which placed limits on how large a local farming community could grow, and this more than any other factor determined the shape of the communities within which most people lived. Seventy-four per cent of the population are shown as living in rural settlements, in ' villages and hamlets ', in Gregory King's survey of England in 1688. Within the limits of these communities — minute by modern standards — the great majority of people were born and lived out their lives. This is not to say that people necessarily spent all of their lives in the same village: some would leave in search of work; others would leave as part of larger movements of population in times of economic distress or social upheaval. But the fundamental character of the villages and rural settlements scattered throughout England was not altered by the extent to which their populations were able to move from one such settlement to another. It was only the gentry, five per cent or less of the population, who were able to live in a larger world. For the greater part of the rest of the population a community of three, four or five hundred people determined the boundary of their world, the basic unit of social life.[23] If a history of homosexuality in this period is to record the experiences of more than a small minority of people, then it is there, within the borders of a village, a group of hamlets or a single parish, that we must look first.

It should not therefore come as a surprise when, as we try to piece together the place homosexuality occupied in society, its social expression appears hemmed in by the size of the villages and towns within which the great mass of people lived, despite the obvious dangers of a small and disapproving community. James Slater was a barber who appeared at the Hertfordshire Assizes in 1607 charged with sodomy; the relationship which had been his undoing had been with the son of a neighbour, despite the danger this must clearly have involved.[24] Similarly Matthew Heaton, a clergyman in East Grinstead, was prosecuted at the Sussex Assizes in 1580, if the indictment is to be believed, because of the homosexual relationship he had had with a boy in his parish.[25] However difficult, for the great majority of people homosexuality was not — could not be — a relationship with a stranger or a casual acquaintance: it was overwhelmingly something which took place between neighbours and friends. When John Wilson the vicar of Arlington in Sussex was ejected from his benefice in 1643, the charges brought against him included the claim that ' divers times [he] attempted to commit buggery with Nathaniel Brown, Samuel Andrews and Robert Williams, his parishoners '[26]. The terms of the charge are revealing in themselves, but there is also an interesting companion to them in the depositions made on the occasion the year before when John Wilson had been the subject of a complaint to the Justices of the Peace. The complaint had been about his political views not his unorthodox sexual behaviour, but it contains a revealing vignette of him passing a Sunday afternoon ' in company ' at the house of one of his parishioners in July 1642 with some local farmers and agricultural workers, one of his own servants and a Puritan tailor, with whom he quarrelled about politics.[27] Gentry though he was, his social life was circumscribed by the size of the rural community within which he lived. Is it therefore surprising that the scope of his sexual life should have been circumscribed? The limits of the local community were a fundamental influence on the limits of social life, and what was true of social life in general was equally true of sexual relations. It is where the relationship of society and homosexuality began.

The limits of the local community were, then, a major barrier within which the great majority of people lived their lives. But it was not the only one; there was also a second, less public but no less important: the household. Together with the local community it represented one of the two principal restrictions on the possible scope of an individual's life. But it is only since the late 1960s that we have been able to form an accurate picture of what the household in pre-industrial England was like. The key, largely unrecognised as such until then, lay in the wealth of data on the human facts of everyday life in the period after the Reformation preserved in English parish records. This data is partly in the form of registers of births, marriages and deaths, which are by and large very well kept for long periods, and partly in the form of lists of local inhabitants compiled at particular dates. Both registers and population lists, but especially the latter, have now been analysed as length by Peter Laslett and the Cambridge Group for the History of Population and Social Structure. The result has been to drastically revise opinions on this subject. It has also complicated them, in that the household in pre-industrial England as it now appears is both familiar and unfamiliar depending on what aspect one is looking at. In its structure it is still essentially the same now as it was then and has been so since at least the beginning of the sixteenth century, the earliest period for which extensive records are available: the norm then, as now, was a household consisting of two generations living together under the same roof without collateral relatives. And, as is also the case today, a member of the second generation was more likely to found a household of his own — it was men not women who founded households — than to inherit that of his parents; when the children of the family were ready to marry, they would generally leave to establish their own homes. The 'extended' family of several generations and branches living together in one household — accepted by earlier historians as the norm — was a myth, as far as Western Europe at least was concerned. The presence in the household of aunts and uncles, of aged grandparents and tiny children, which is the traditional picture — an image of emotional stability and peaceful order — seems now, in the light of the quite divergent conclusions to be derived from statistical analysis of population lists, to represent views on what ought to have been the case rather than what actually was.[28] It should be said though that this does not preclude a household taking an extended form for some part of its existence. And 'household' is not synonymous with 'family'. Statistical analysis can tell us how many people on average lived in the same household and how they were likely to have been related to each other: what it cannot tell us is to what extent they thought of that unit in the same way that we do of the family today. Certainly the role of external influences — influences of clan, community or state — has changed significantly and had probably done so by the end of the seventeenth century.[29] But conceived of in the immediate terms of the number and relationship of people living together under one roof, the sixteenth-century household as an institution did not differ substantially from its twentieth-century counterpart.

There are though some reservations to be made. Two in particular concern areas which will have an important bearing on the subject of this book. One concerns the authority of the head of the household. An important element in the make-up of the household was that it was a profoundly patriarchal institution, both in relation to the subordination of women and in the authority exercised by the head of the household over its servants. There is a graphic illustration of this in the number of reports of servants being maltreated — often brutally and for long periods — that abound in any Quarter Sessions' records; they are an eloquent testimony of how extensive was the effective authority of the master of the household. The second reservation is less dramatic but in the long run no less important; it concerns these servants themselves. By modern standards the population of England in the sixteenth and seventeenth centuries contained an immense number of servants: 13.4 per cent of the population in Laslett and Wall's survey of one hundred pre-industrial communities were servants, and — what is even more striking — there were one or more servants in no less than 28.5 per cent of the households looked at.[30] With figures of this size, this was clearly an institution that affected more than the gentry alone; the yeoman farmer, the blacksmith, even on occasions the humble drover or smallholder would quite likely have shared their homes with one or more servants. In view of how widespread this institution was among different social groups including both the wealthy and the relatively poor, it is highly improbable that such an army of servants consisted of domestic servants in the modern sense. What then were they? Part of the explanation is provided by the statistics themselves. If the number of servants in a population is related to the number of children in the same population and its average age of first marriage, there is a recognisable correspondence. The proportion of servants in these communities is negatively related to the proportion of children in the same population, i.e. the more individuals who appear as children in a list the less the number that appear as servants and vice versa.[31] Also if the numbers of servants and of married people in the same age groups are compared, it is clear that it would have been rare indeed for a servant to have been married.[32] The explanation is that the servants in a household were the children of poorer households accumulating through their wages sufficient capital to establish households of their own, an event which would coincide with marriage. The rest of the explanation lies in the nature of a pre-industrial economy. Since the nineteenth century manufacturing has largely been a question of factory work, and we are naturally accustomed to thinking of the two as being connected. But this was not the case in seventeenth-century England. Before the coming of industrialisation, manufacturing was carried on as much in the house as in the workshop; and the dividing line between the two was often unclear. A mill or a forge, a tailor's shop or the work of a farm would often have been part and parcel of the life of the household, the labour for this being provided by the members of the household themselves: the householder, his wife and children. Where this was insufficient — as it often would have been — the solution was to take into the household the children of more humble homes, nominally as servants but occupying a similar position and doing the same work as the children themselves with whom they now lived. When eventually they were able to found households of their own, they would marry and leave — servants and children alike. In the meantime, unless they were formally apprenticed, they might move from house to house, but their social and economic position would be the same in each case. Whether spent in their parents' home or in the adopted home of a master, it was a stage of life which a great many people would have known.[33]

An institution of this kind clearly had important implications for the sexual life of the many unmarried men and women who lived in a setting which was both their home and their place of work, whether as children of the household or its servants. This is especially evident when one considers how large a part of an individual's sexual life must have been affected. It was rare for a man to start a household of his own before his late twenties, and this might well have been delayed until his early thirties. The average age of marriage for a woman would have been rather earlier, generally in her early twenties.[34] While it is very difficult now to discover what the age of sexual maturity was,[35] clearly it would have been well before this; and the constraints of the household would have governed a significant part of many individuals' lives long after puberty. For an unmarried servant living and working under the close discipline of a master in the same setting and with the same people, the confines of the household might be expected to have put a severe limitation on the available sexual contacts. It is an expectation which analysis has borne out, although so far the research has been largely in terms of heterosexuality. G.R. Quaife has analysed the depositions in the Somerset Court of Quarter Sessions 1645-1660 arising out of the Justices' bastardy jurisdiction; the most common circumstance in the cases he looked at concerned sexual relations between a female servant and someone living in the same household.[36] E.S. Morgan's similar study of the Middlesex County Court in Puritan Massachusetts, although lacking in statistical data, came to similar conclusions.[37] But in such circumstances homosexual relations were no less subject to these restrictions than heterosexual ones. And for an unmarried servant homosexuality had certain advantages: it was less likely to arouse the interest of the local Justices of the Peace. While sodomy cases appear only rarely in Quarter Sessions records,[38] these courts took a lively interest in cases of premarital heterosexual intercourse. It is not difficult to see the reason why: one of the principal preoccupations of the Justices of the Peace was to see that illegitimate children did not fall on the poor rate. There was then considerable pressure on an unmarried servant to find alternative sexual outlets; homosexuality was one of these, an alternative made easier by the common practice of male servants sleeping together. Also the restrictions of the household being what they were, it was in any case a good deal easier for a male servant to have homosexual relations with someone living in the same household than it would have been to seek such a relationship outside. An illustration of this, which probably came to court because of the coercion involved, is the prosecution of a labourer, Meredith Davy of Minehead in Somerset, at the Somerset Court of Quarter Sessions in 1630. According to the evidence of his master's apprentice, a boy 'aged twelve years or thereabouts' called John Vicary, with whom he shared a bed, Davy had been in the habit of having sexual relations with the boy on Sunday and holiday nights after he had been drinking; eventually the boy cried out and Davy ended up before the Justices.[39] Similarly John Swan and John Litster, who were charged with sodomy in Edinburgh in 1570, are described in the record of their trial as being smiths and servants of the same master.[40] In both of these instances, a familiar social institution is clearly recognisable.

Meredith Davy's relationship with the apprentice he had shared a bed with is more complex though than the simple accident of their living in the same household. The young apprentice would have had a lower standing in the household than Davy, who was an adult; and it was presumably this which encouraged him — wrongly as it turned out — to think that he could take advantage of the boy. It is an important point. In a household of any substantial size the distinction in their status would have been only one of a series of such distinctions; it was part of the nature of the household itself. The household was a hierarchical institution, in which each of its members had a clearly defined position. It was also a patriarchal institution, in which the pre-eminent position was that of the master; and the distinction in status between master and servant was in some respects a model for distinctions between the servants themselves. The patriarchal nature of the household was as powerful a factor impinging on the lives of the people who lived within it as was its restriction as a social unit. This is not to say that the sixteenth-century household was necessarily governed by a man. It is not male supremacy as such which is involved but rather what that implies. In the absence of a suitable male it could on occasion be headed by a woman. But its nature — if not invariably its form —was characteristically patriarchal, allowing some of the individuals within it — and one in particular — a considerable degree of power over the lives of the others.

It is not surprising then that it had a powerful influence on social relations and particularly — and this is my principal concern here — on sexual relations, heterosexual and homosexual alike. The most common form, for example, in which bastardy cases appear in the courts is that of a female servant who has had sexual relations with the master of the household or the master's son.[41] There is also considerable evidence, although of a somewhat different kind — it is not a topic in which JPs showed much interest — of homosexual as well as heterosexual relationships being common between masters and servants, to the extent that this seems to have been a widespread institution. It figures in both the major homosexual scandals of the seventeenth century: that of Francis Bacon and that of Mervyn Touchet, second Earl of Castlehaven. Francis Bacon was apparently in the habit of having sexual relations with his male servants; this would probably have gone unnoticed had it not been for his prodigal generosity to them, which was the subject of a good deal of disapproving comment. The evidence is partly the malicious gossip reported by John Aubrey and Sir Simonds D'Ewes;[42] but the stories are borne out by a letter from Francis Bacon's mother to another son, Anthony Bacon, complaining about his brother's servants and especially his keeping 'that bloody Percy, as I told him then, yea as a coach companion and bed companion'.[43] Similar circumstances appear in the record of the trial of the Earl of Castlehaven in 1631. He was charged with sodomy and assisting in the rape of his wife, and at the trial several of his male servants gave evidence that he had been in the habit of having sexual relations with them. It was rare for a charge of this kind to come to the courts, and the evident prejudice against Castlehaven because of his Roman Catholicism makes one suspect the whole proceedings; it is also possible that the rape of his wife — by one of his favourites — may also have singled him out for unusual treatment. Whatever one may feel about the case as a whole however, there is no reason to doubt that he regularly had sexual relations with his male servants; their detailed evidence is sufficiently convincing.[44]

As well as these two *causes célèbres*, homosexual relations between masters and their servants were bitterly complained of by the satirists. In *The Black Book* (probably by Thomas Middleton) a sodomite is said to keep a 'page, which fills up the place of an ingle'.[45] 'Lustful catamites' are one of the 'private parasites' complained of in Richard Brathwaite's *Placentia*.[46] It is also something which appears on several occasions in the poems of John Wilmot:

Then give me health, wealth, mirth, and wine,
  And, if busy love entrenches,
There's a sweet, soft page of mine
  Does the trick worth forty wenches.[47]

And in his *The Disabled Debauchee* the speaker reminisces:

Nor shall our love-fits, Chloris, be forgot,
  When each the well-looked linkboy strove t'enjoy,
And the best kiss was the deciding lot
  Whether the boy fucked you, or I the boy.[48]

(A linkboy was a boy employed to carry a 'link', i.e. a light, to show the way along the street.)

It is also significant that when John Wilmot adapted Fletcher's *Valentinian* for the conventions of the Restoration stage he removed the passage in which Valentinian's favourite the eunuch Lycias is shown to be of noble birth, leaving the impression (which a Restoration audience would have been more accustomed to) that he was his servant and no more.[49] There are, though, difficulties in interpreting this material, John Wilmot in the Restoration as much as the earlier Jacobean satirists. This is partly because the literary references are so highly coloured by the concerns of these writers and partly because of the scarcity of material on this point in court records. John Wilmot was writing for an aristocratic audience; and as far as the Jacobean satirists were concerned homosexual relations between servants and their masters were only an incidental detail in their principal purpose, to libel the London gentry.

As for the courts, it was not something that concerned them greatly unless violence was involved;[50] a Quarter Sessions case with sadistic overtones which may have been of this kind is that of Richard Finch a London merchant, who was called before the Middlesex Justices in 1609 charged with abusing his servant Nicholas Wheeler and 'correcting him unreasonably with whipcords, being quite naked'.[51] But a case like this is rare: the courts were apparently unconcerned with sexual relations between masters and servants unless a scandal was involved or an illegitimate child was produced. The result is that the evidence is disproportionately weighted by a concern with the upper classes. But it would be seriously wrong to assume that servants were a common feature only in such households: there were far too many of them for that. In the population list for Ealing in 1599, published by Laslett and Wall, of the 85 households in the village a staggering 34.2 per cent of them contained one or more servants, and that out of a total population of only 427.[52] The patriarchal household with its servants was an institution that touched the lives of an immense number of people. Whether two workmen in the household of the same master in Edinburgh, or a labourer sleeping with a young apprentice in seventeenth-century Somerset, or a London merchant having homosexual relations with his servants in the relative security of his own household, it was an institution that necessarily influenced the sexual lives of those who lived within it.

The household was the classic form of patriarchy, but it was not the only one. It was also an influential model, or perhaps rather one should say the clearest form of an element present throughout society. Probably the most obvious example of this is the relationship of pupil and teacher. The teacher stood to the child *in loco parentis,* with some of the authority over his children and servants due to the master of the household; and there is reason to think that the educational system, as well as the household, involved forms of institutionalised homosexuality. This was particularly likely at the universities, where an unmarried and supposedly celibate college fellow would customarily share his room with a number of young male students.[53] The likely consequences of this very much exercised the author of *The Times' Whistle,* as he explains at length in his passage on the evils of sodomy. With the marginal note 'I grieve at the vices which prevail at the universities' he protests:

How many towardly young gentlemen
(Instead of ink, with tears I fill my pen
To write it) sent unto thee by their friends
For art and education, the true ends
Their parents aim at, are with this infection
Poisoned by them whose best protection
Should keep them from all sin! Alack the while
Each pedant tutor should his pupil spoil!

Because 'this vice is so inveterate', and 'grown to so strong a custom', he gloomily concludes that it is hardly likely to be discouraged.[54] A similar complaint was made by John Marston, whom the author of *The Times' Whistle* had probably read and who blamed the homosexuality apparent at the universities on

Papist missionaries returning from Catholic seminaries abroad:

> Hence, hence, ye falsed, seeming patriots.
> Return not with pretence of salving spots,
> When here ye soil us with impurity
> And monstrous filth of Douai seminary.
> What though Iberia yield you liberty
> To snort in source of Sodom villainy?
> What though the blooms of young nobility,
> Committed to your Rodon's custody,
> Yee Nero-like abuse? Yet near approach
> Your new St Omer's lewdness here to broach,
> Tainting our towns and hopeful academies
> With your lust-baiting most abhorred means ...
> Had I some snout-fair brats, they should endure
> The new found Castilian calenture
> Before some pedant-tutor in his bed
> Should use my fry like Phrygian Ganymede.[55]

It is not wholly clear what part of the educational system Marston is referring to, whether the universities alone or whether he had schoolmasters in mind also; but there is evidence that homosexuality was institutionalised not only at the universities but also in grammar schools and even in the village schools. The limited effect which complaints about this had is revealing of how deep-rooted the institution was. In 1541 Nicholas Udall, who was headmaster of Eton at the time, was involved in a scandal because of the homosexual relationship he had had with one of his former pupils. The events are somewhat mysterious, but the affair seems to have come to light during an investigation by the Privy Council into the theft of some school plate in which the boy had been involved. A similar scandal, with — as we shall see — a similar outcome, involved the schoolmaster of Great Tey in Essex, a certain Mr Cooke who was presented in the ecclesiastical court in 1594 as 'a man of beastly behaviour amongst his scholars' and one who 'teacheth them all manner of bawdry'. In each case the complaints about homosexuality had little effect. The Privy Council were obviously concerned about Udall's possible role in the theft, and he was dismissed as headmaster and spent a short time in prison; but it is indicative of the degree to which homosexuality was effectively tolerated in the educational system that neither Udall nor Cooke suffered any permanent loss. Cooke failed to appear to answer the charge, and nothing further seems to have occurred; Udall continued his career with his reputation apparently undamaged. In neither case did a charge of homosexuality in this context do any permanent harm.[56]

A third area where homosexuality appears to have been institutionalised and tacitly tolerated was homosexual prostitution, and there is substantial evidence that this was an important part of the sexual life at least of London well into the second half of the seventeenth century. There is an incidental reference to this in one of John Donne's *Satires*, particularly significant in that the minor details of these are always unusually sharp and reliable. The profligate young man who is the subject of Donne's first *Satire* (published in the early 1590s) is taken to task by the speaker because, among his many other vices:

> ...thou...dost not only approve
> But, in rank itchy lust, desire and love
> The nakedness and bareness to enjoy
> Of thy plump muddy whore or prostitute boy.[57]

The familiar sight of the 'prostitute boy' in Renaissance London is the origin of the distinctive equivalents John Florio gives for 'catamíto' in his 1611 Italian/English dictionary:

> Catamíto, *one hired to sin against nature, an ingle, a ganymede.*[58]

He apparently took these to be equivalent terms. There is also reason to think that homosexual prostitution existed in elaborate and developed forms as well as the more straightforward. Alongside the casual prostitution of the streets and public places — which is the least this could have referred to — there is evidence of more sophisticated forms and in particular of the existence of homosexual brothels. John Marston included a condemnation of 'male stews' (i.e. male brothels) in his *Scourge of Villanie* published in 1598,[59] and Clement Walker's *Relations and Observations* contains a mention in passing of several newly built homosexual brothels in London in late 1649.[60] Neither Clement Walker nor John Marston, however, describes in any detail what these brothels were like; and we should probably not think of them as brothels in the strict sense of the word, visualising commercial establishments more or less exclusively concerned with homosexual prostitution. If the parallels with heterosexual prostitution are a guide — and there certainly are such parallels[61] — these are more likely to have been taverns (which could earn notorious reputations) where prostitutes were able to entertain their clients. Such taverns, together with young male prostitutes walking the streets and alleys of Elizabethan London, probably offer the principal way we should envisage homosexual prostitution in the London of the time.

There is though a further form of homosexual prostitution which it is possible to distinguish, and there are parallels with heterosexual prostitution here also: the young man living in a household, nominally with the status of a servant but having a relationship with the master of the household with strong overtones of prostitution. This might be a matter of no more than a few days, as in John Marston's description of the sodomite whose personal servant — apparently a page — is really a prostitute who has been 'closely' i.e. secretly hired:

> But ho, what Ganymede is that doth grace
> The gallant's heels, one who for two days' space
> Is closely hired?[62]

It might also be a matter lasting weeks, months, or even years. This is presumably part of what Middleton, Brathwaite and Wilmot, quoted earlier in a different context, had in mind; their pages and 'private parasites' seem to have been prostitutes, albeit established in the household, as much as they were servants. It also partly explains the ambivalent position of some of the young men in the households of Francis Bacon and the Earl of Castlehaven: it is not clear whether these young men were servants or a kind of domestic prostitute, and perhaps one would be wrong to try and make a sharp distinction between the two. The relationship between client and prostitute — as indeed between teacher and pupil — had obvious analogies with the basic and influential relationship of master and servant; in the domestic prostitute the two are hardly distinguishable.

Another — but more specialised — form of prostitution existed in connection with the London playhouses. This is not surprising. The Elizabethan and Jacobean theatre acquired a reputation for homosexuality, as Philip Stubbes graphically claimed.[63] It was also a claim made by Edward Guilpin in similar terms in his *Skialetheia,* which describes a sodomite as someone 'who is at every play and every night sups with his ingles';[64] and it is repeated in Michael Drayton's *The Moone-Calfe*, where the theatres are denounced as one of the haunts of the sodomite.[65] Given the prevalence of homosexuality in the theatrical milieu and the importance of prostitution in London generally, it is understandable that homosexual prostitution should have taken root in a distinctive way in the theatres. In particular, it seems that at times an actor's relationship with his patron could have overtones of homosexuality and prostitution: such at least is the implication in Lucy Hutchinson's famous comment on the change in the Court after the death of James I:

> The face of the Court was much changed in the change of the king, for King Charles was temperate, chaste, and serious; so that the fools and bawds, mimics and catamites of the former court grew out of fashion and the nobility and courtiers, who did not quite abandon their debaucheries, yet so reverenced the king as to retire into corners to practice them.[66]

'Fools and bawds, mimics and catamites' — the expression is difficult now to construe, but it clearly has overtones of the theatre and of prostitution. 'Fools' here are obviously jesters, but the theatrical reference is sharper in its parallel 'mimics'. A 'mimic' was a burlesque actor; the usage is now obsolete but was current in the early seventeenth century and is here the only reading of the word that fits easily.[67] As regards prostitution, the parallel between 'bawds' and 'catamites' suggests that 'catamites' is being used with the same connotation as in John Florio's dictionary. And there is evidence that it was not only in the relations of actors and their patrons in the court circles that homosexuality was involved; the actors had distinctions in status of their own; some of them indeed were only boys. When in Ben Jonson's play *Poetaster* the elder Ovid learns that his son is to become an actor, his response is: 'What? Shall I have my son a stager now, an ingle for players'?[68] The parallel with the homosexuality of the household is striking — both as between master and servants and between servants of different status. Changed and elaborated though it was, there is still discernible here — as in other forms of homosexuality in the society of the time — the powerful influence of a basic model: the patriarchal household of master and mistress, servants and children.

What is missing is any social expression of homosexuality based on the fact of homosexuality itself. To a late twentieth-century observer accustomed to the idea of a distinctive homosexual subculture amounting to a minority community it is a striking absence. It is not that we lack the material to reconstruct the ways homosexuality and society were related; there is abundant evidence in the period we have been looking at, stretching from the close of the Middle Ages into the second half of the seventeenth century, of the forms of social life in which homosexuality appeared. What we look for in vain are any features peculiar to it alone. And the social forms it did take, within the confines of small rural communities and the patriarchal structure of the household — a structure discernible also in a series of parallel relationships throughout society — had their origin elsewhere. But there was a common element. What determined the shared and recurring features of homosexual relationships was the prevailing distribution of power, economic power and social power, not the fact of homosexuality itself. It is a crucial realisation. At first sight the place homosexuality occupied in the society of Renaissance England is apt not to seem very dissimilar to that of our own: many of its institutions and problems are easily recognisable; and the ways of making love do not change over the centuries. But as we piece together its relationship to the rest of society and as — rather later — we begin to discern institutions for which there is now no conceivable parallel whatsoever, that sense of familiarity wanes and the full dimensions of the change which has occurred begin to become apparent.

But are there not some more immediate questions that along the way have gone unanswered? An analysis of this kind — of society as a whole, of its structures and characteristic forms of life — does not tell us how it appeared from the viewpoint of someone living within it. In particular it does not tell us how the problems of a homosexual relationship would have appeared to the people whose daily lives were affected by it at the turn of the sixteenth century. And without this are we not in danger of missing something perhaps very important? That unsettling question is reinforced by what by now will probably have become unavoidably and disturbingly apparent: an analysis of this kind, if that is all we are to have, is going to leave us with some very strange paradoxes indeed. Is it not surprising that the writers quoted in the first chapter of this book should have spoken of sodomites in terms so far removed from their everyday experience, as the companions of witches and werewolves, as agents of the King of Spain, when for most if not all of them their actual experience of homosexuality would have been primarily in terms of someone who lived in the same village or town or even under the same roof? And how are we to square the profound, the metaphysical fear of homosexuality they express with its complex elaboration throughout society in a variety of forms? How is it to be reconciled with the tacit acceptance of homosexual prostitution and of institutionalised homosexuality in the household and educational system? Clearly something very important is missing, and the approach adopted so far is not going to produce it. We need to ask a different question.

Chapter Three:

Society
and the Individual

Society is a process. It is more than social institutions and cultural forms, which is how a past society is apt to appear to the eye of the historian. The justification for describing it in such terms is that they highlight the common and recurring elements in its way of life: they work because they are simplifications. But like all simplications they are also and necessarily a distortion of reality, for this is not how society appears from within. From the viewpoint of the individual within it, the structure of society is largely obscured. To the extent that it is ever directly experienced, it is through an innumerable series of formative experiences; some perhaps are crucial, but many are no more than minute adjustments to the problems of everyday life as these obtrude themselves on the individual. These adjustments are what bridge the potential gap between our perception of the world around us and its reality, or rather they are what can do so. They are thus the source of a social factor as open to historical and cultural variation as other more noticeable ones, and in the study of homosexuality in Renaissance England it is this factor which on examination proves to be the most important of all.[1]

But where are we to begin? That problem at least is easily solved, for if there was one characteristic of homosexuality which must surely have influenced behaviour more than any other then that is the revulsion and violent hostility which homosexuality aroused. It will be worth looking at this in some detail, as it forms the basis of any understanding of the social pressures which shaped homosexual relationships.

> Die villains die, O more than infamous
> Foul monsters...
> Drown, drown the hell-hounds, and revenge the wrong
> Which they have done our Mother Nature long.[2]

This venom is not the work of some crude pamphleteer or rabble-rouser; the writer is none other than Guillaume de Saluste Sieur du Bartas in Josua Sylvester's translation, the very model of Protestant humanism, whose didactic poem on the Creation and early history of the world (from which this quotation is taken) occupied an honoured place in many households alongside the Bible and Foxe's *Acts and Monuments*. Its ideas had a wide coinage, and his attitude to homosexuality is as violent and unpleasant as that of any of his contemporaries. His lingering description of the death-agony of Sodom and Gomorrah is as revealing of his readers' state of mind as of his own:

> Here one perceiving the next chamber burning,
> With sudden leap towards the window turning,
> Thinks to cry 'fire!'; but instantly the smoke
> And flame without his voice within do choke.
> Another sooner feels than sees the fire,
> For while (O horror) in the stinking mire
> Of his foul lust he lies a lightning flash
> Him and his love at once to dust doth dash:
> The abhored bed is burnt, and they as well
> Coupled in plague as sin are sent to Hell.
> Another yet on tops of houses crawls,
> But his foot slips and down at last he falls.
> Another feeling all his clothes afire,
> Thinking to quench them ere it should come nigher,
> Leaps in a lake; but all the lake began
> To boil and bubble like a seething pan...[3]

It is a sadistic description and a characteristic one. Du Bartas was the spokesman for a culture in which homosexuality was a loathsome and evil thing: the horror of the sodomites' deaths was in his eyes a fitting counterpart to the horror of their lives.

All too often a quite different impression has been given. The Renaissance concern for classical ideals was taken by the homosexual reformers of the late nineteenth century and their successors as implying a tolerant attitude to homosexuality, an openness in this respect in sharp contrast to the narrowness of medieval Catholic Europe.[4] It was a persuasive myth, but it was not sound history. The broadening of the human spirit this implied had more to do with the desire for law reform in nineteenth-century England than with the actuality of Renaissance Europe, whose attitudes as far as homosexuality was concerned were directly derived with little change from late medieval times. Its literary support was spurious. It consisted of the conventions of Platonic friendship and of exercises which on analysis turn out to be based on classical models. This was attractive material of course, especially in a society such as Victorian England where classical ideals were accorded a high degree of respect; but it was far from being evidence of attitudes to homosexuality. Thomas Browne could write of his longing to be in the arms of his friend, and add a few pages later: 'that part of our noble friends that we love is not that part that we embrace but that insensible part that our arms cannot embrace.'[5] He would have been astonished at the suggestion that the rarified and Platonic friendship of which he was writing could have been construed as having anything to do with homosexuality. Thomas Browne was at least genuinely advocating a spiritual ideal, but very often such expressions elsewhere seem hardly more than a formal convention. The poet William Drummond is a case in point. His published work contains conventionally elegant verses on subjects such as 'Ganymede the fair' or the love of the shepherds Alexis and Damon.[6] But the manuscripts which were not published in his lifetime — and which are a good deal more earthy and personal — are in part explicitly about homosexuality; and these are written in quite different terms. Homosexuality as he puts it is part of all those things which are 'polluted and unclean . . . all that is beastly and obscene'.[7] It is not difficult to see what Drummond's attitude to homosexuality actually was.

It would be anachronistic and naive to see a validation of homosexual love in the writings of Thomas Browne or William Drummond; but just such a misreading — and a serious one — has been made with the writings of Richard Barnfield, who has been claimed as a poet of outspoken homosexual love.[8] As a young man Richard Barnfield published a number of poems taken up with passionate declarations of male love, addressed principally in conventional terms to 'Ganymede'.[9] The speaker is usually anonymous, but in the longest of these poems (the *Affectionate Shepherd*) this passionate declaration of love is that of a lovesick Arcadian shepherd. These poems have a good deal of charm and are certainly more touching than the verses of William Drummond, but there is no reason to think that they are any the less literary exercises. As Richard Barnfield himself explained:

> Some there were that did interpret *The Affectionate Shepherd* otherwise than in truth I meant, touching the subject thereof to wit the love of a shepherd to a boy; a fault the which I will not excuse, because I never made. Only this I will unshadow my conceit: being nothing else but an imitation of Vergil in the second Eclogue, of Alexis.[10]

That this is indeed the truth is suggested by Richard Barnfield's commonplace book:[11] the manuscript of this was never intended for publication and is both robustly pornographic and entirely heterosexual. It reveals Richard Barnfield's personality as it actually was, and is far removed in its sexual interests from the delicate sensibility of the *Affectionate Shepherd*. The freshness and immediacy of these poems is the result of Richard Barnfield's skill, and it is this which has led to the assumption — which should never be made with Elizabethan or Jacobean poetry without independent support — that they are the product of personal experience. Like other self-consciously classical poetry of this kind they were the product of a literary genre which (if it was more than a mere exercise) was about friendship, the 'insensible part' of love, not sexuality but a Platonic meeting of minds. It was not about homosexuality. Attitudes to homosexuality had hardly changed since the thirteenth century; it was in the Renaissance as it was then, a horror, a thing to be unreservedly execrated.

It is difficult to appreciate the weight of that condemnation if one has not had to read through — as the researcher must — the constant repetition of expressions of revulsion and horror, of apologies for the very mention of the subject that it was felt necessary to express whenever was mentioned the 'detestable and abominable sin, amongst Christians not to be named':[12]

> Whose vice in special, if I would declare,
> It were enough for to perturb the air.[13]

I cover it with reverence and trembling that ... [14]

These are but tricks of youth; now arm your ears
With patience for to hear of pallid fears:
Suppose a devil from the infernal pit ... [15]

... (things fearful to name) ... [16]

   Forbear, dear younglings, pray awhile forbear.
Stand farther from me, or else stop your ear,
At the obscene sound of the unbeseeming words
Which to my Muse this odious place affords;
Or, if its horror cannot drive you hence,
Hearing their sin pray hear their punishments.
   These beastly men ... [17]

Phrases such as these, all of which are a preamble to a mention of homosexuality or a comment on it, say little more than had been said a score of times before, and are rightly pared away by historians when they assemble their material; but it is their constant repetition that brings home to what extent they were looked for and how much of a consensus they represented. Of course these expressions did not necessarily represent the personal views of their authors; they often seem no more than mere formulas, added almost dutifully. But they are all the more revealing for that of what attitude was expected and of what someone if pressed was likely to say, of what in effect represented the 'common sense' view.

And that 'common sense' view was that homosexuality was an abomination. Renaissance Platonism left it intact, and it is difficult to exaggerate the fear and loathing of homosexuality to be read in the literature of the time. Except for a short period under Mary, homosexuality was a felony punishable by death throughout the period this book is concerned with. Taken cold it is difficult to account for the violence of this hostility, but in the context of the myths surrounding homosexuality which have already been discussed it is more explicable: in them it was part of an anarchy that threatened to engulf the established order, even the very stars in their courses. Could there be a greater horror or one more deserving of unrelenting hostility? It is in this light that we should understand the solemn charge of James VI of Scotland — later James I of England — to his son that homosexuality was one of the few 'horrible crimes' that a king was 'bound in conscience never to forgive'.[18]

The mythical element was also the nub of the problem for the individual who was still drawn to homosexuality despite the crushing disapproval of society at large. He was faced with more than the naked fact of that intense disapproval: he had also to contend with its widely accepted integration into the way the scheme of things was understood and into the Christianity of his time. It was this dimension which was the iron in the problem, especially as that view of things was probably something he shared himself. To meet the problem head-on entailed seeing the world in a very different way from what was usual and easy.

The problems in doing this were immense, and yet there is evidence that some individuals did overcome them. One of the most interesting and certainly the most famous was the playwright Christopher Marlowe, whose outspoken views on homosexuality — and the fraudulent claims of religion — have already been referred to.[19] The principal source for these, the reports of the informer Richard Baines, do need though to be used with caution, as he carefully arranged his material to fit the preconceptions of the authorities to whom he was reporting. But some crucial details can be independently verified, and there is other evidence of Marlowe's 'atheism'. Baines's depositions should then be taken as documents which have been carefully constructed but which are none the less based on Marlowe's actual opinions. Baines however gives the impression that Marlowe was an atheist and 'blasphemer' pure and simple, but this is probably misleading. A sceptic he certainly was, but probably not an atheist, at least not in the modern sense. His views are more likely to have been akin to those of Sir Walter Raleigh, to whose circle Marlowe was connected:

'In his speech on the scaffold,' wrote John Aubrey in his life of Walter Raleigh, 'I heard my cousin Whitney say (and I think 'tis printed) that he spake not one word of Christ but of the great and incomprehensible God, with much zeal and adoration, so that he concluded that he was an a-Christ not an atheist.'[20] In Raleigh's circle this Socinianism was accompanied by a thorough-going scepticism of conventional religion akin to many of Marlowe's views as Baines reports them. Additional evidence is given for this view by the presence of a Socinian treatise amongst Marlowe's belongings, which later passed into the possession of Thomas Kyd and was found when Kyd was arrested. It is in this context that we should read the 'blasphemy' attributed to Marlowe by both Baines and Kyd that Christ and St John were lovers:

> He would report St John to be Our Saviour Christ's Alexis. I cover it with reverence and trembling that is that Christ did love him with an extraordinary love [Kyd].[21]

> A note containing the opinion of one Christopher Marlowe, concerning his damnable judgement of religion and scorn of God's word . . . that St John the Evangelist was bedfellow to Christ and leaned always in his bosom; that he used him as the sinners of Sodoma [Baines].[22]

This claim — one Marlowe often made judging by the fact that Kyd and Baines independently report it — is of a pattern with several others reported by Baines which also set Christ's evidently human life in ironic contrast to the claim that he was divine. This is Socinianism, and adds up to a radical rejection of the Christianity of his day. Marlowe's defiant assertion of homosexuality which Baines also attributes to him came from the same source. What made it possible was Marlowe's thorough-going rejection of the intellectual current of his time. It was a radical and dangerous solution to the generally shared disapproval of homosexuality, but it was a possible solution none the less.

Marlowe's comments on Christ and St John refer indirectly to another but less drastic means of escaping the full cultural weight of Renaissance Christianity's condemnation of homosexual relations. While Marlowe apparently rejected orthodox Christianity root and branch, one of the terms he uses alludes to an alternative that did not require as strenuous a mental adjustment as outright scepticism. It is the word 'Alexis'. The influence of both Kyd and Baines is clearly present in the way these comments are reported, but there is good reason to think that the use of the term 'Alexis' in this context is Marlowe's own. The Alexis referred to is the beautiful youth loved by the shepherd Corydon in Vergil's second Eclogue; so positive, if not exquisite, a context for Marlowe's blasphemy was hardly likely to have been provided by Kyd: Kyd's object in recounting Marlowe's 'monstrous opinions' to the authorities was to demonstrate that he himself was innocent and that Marlowe was the villain. When we find Kyd using a term such as this he is more likely to be reporting Marlowe's expression than creating his own; and the supposition is strengthened by Marlowe's poem *The*

Passionate Shepherd to His Love,[23] which A.L. Rowse believes was modelled on Vergil's second Eclogue.[24]

Kyd was a man broken by torture, and removed from his 'reverence and trembling' Vergil's poem represented a whole set of values far indeed from those of the Elizabethans. It was one of several such classical texts which were easily available and yet contained a validation of homosexuality at odds with Renaissance prejudice, and Alexis only one of several such figures. An appreciation of Vergil did not require a break with Christianity, but the revival of classical culture could not help but suggest the possibility of values existing different from those prevailing. This was not necessarily intended; apparently homosexual themes in Renaissance literature need to be treated with extreme caution. But a writer's intention does not delimit the range of responses readers can bring for themselves, and the revival of classical culture could be taken by an individual who was determined to do so as opening up quite different attitudes to homosexuality. The importance of the distinction between intention and response is that inferences of this kind could as easily then be made when the homosexual reference is used pejoratively as when it is used constructively. The widespread use of the word 'Ganymede' is an example of this. The word is nearly always pejorative, and often refers to nothing more elevated than a male prostitute or a servant kept for sexual purposes; and yet its original meaning, the beautiful boy who was loved by divine Zeus, could never wholly be shaken off. However derogatively used, it was far less threatening than words such as 'sodomite' or 'bugger' with their associations of heresy and hideous retribution, and there was always the possibility of it suggesting attitudes to homosexuality altogether different from the one intended. The use of classical words such as Ganymede (another is paiderastes)[25] or writings such as the second Eclogue was a moral reference point outside Christianity for someone concerned about the sinfulness or otherwise of a homosexual relationship. It was the basis for an adjustment far less dangerous than an outright rejection of Christianity and yet as effective.

Christopher Marlowe of course was a very unusual individual, but there is no reason to think that his scepticism and unconventional frame of reference outside Christianity were unique. Indeed this was part of the stock figure of the sodomite in satirical literature. According to Michael Drayton the sodomite 'counts sacrilege no sin' and 'his blasphemies he useth for his grace',[26] and when John Marston bitterly complains of those who 'magnificate lewd Jovian lust'[27] the context shows that he had the Ganymede myth in mind. Nor should we underestimate the extent to which common people were sceptical about the claims of religion; scepticism of this kind would naturally be more widespread than the contemporary literature which passed the censor suggests. There is a revealing illustration of this in the trial of 'one Plain of Guilford', who was executed at New Haven in 1646, recounted in John Winthrop's *History of New England*:

> ...it was found that being a married man he had committed sodomy with two persons in England and that he had corrupted a great part of the youth of Guilford by masturbations which he had committed and provoked others to the like above a hundred times; and to some who questioned the lawfulness of such a filthy practice he did insinuate seeds of atheism, questioning whether there was a God etc...[28]

Marlowe was not alone in his scepticism.

There was a third way that the individual could justify his behaviour in the face of the prevailing moral code, and that was to rationalise it — or at least to attempt this — within the code's own system of values. It was a mechanism that required a certain amount of self-delusion, but it was an attractive solution. There is an example of this at work in the opinions attributed to the Rev. John Wilson, vicar of Arlington in Sussex, who was ejected by Parliament from his benefice in 1643. John Wilson was no sceptic: his sexual behaviour apart he was an entirely orthodox Laudian clergyman. It was then natural for him to accept conventional values, and when he set out to justify his sexual liasons he did so within their terms. He

> hath professed that he made choice to commit that act with mankind rather than with women to avoid the shame and danger that oft ensueth in begetting bastards... and hath openly affirmed that buggery is no sin.[29]

What he was doing was edging his own sexual behaviour out of what constituted sin, while leaving the category itself intact.

Wilson apparently convinced himself, but was such an eccentric view ever likely to convince anyone else? It is difficult to imagine it doing so. Any specifically intellectual adjustment was bound to be only a limited solution, and this was equally true of one based on the values of classical culture as one based on outright scepticism; for these other mechanisms were just as limited. Classical culture, even when characterised pejoratively, could have influenced only very small numbers of people; and scepticism — though that by no means needed an education — was a very dangerous thing indeed in as absolutist a society as Renaissance England, where politics and religion were so deeply entwined. But probably the greatest difficulty of all in tackling the problem head-on — and this applies equally to all three of these mechanisms — was the sheer size of the mental adjustment they required: some individuals undoubtedly did succeed in overcoming this, but it is difficult to imagine that they were many. And yet somehow the conflict between individual desire and the values of society as a whole had to be resolved, if the desire was to be fulfilled; was there another way?

There was after all a very simple solution, but unfortunately one that later historians would have difficulty in detecting. The individual could simply avoid making the connection; he could keep at two opposite poles the social pressures bearing down on him and his own discordant sexual behaviour, and avoid recognising it for what it was. This may be a difficult idea to grasp. It is not a common-sense view: one assumes that what people do and what they think and say they do bear some relation to each other, deliberate hypocrisy apart. But in some respects this is not always true. In present-day society, for example, homosexual relations are not restricted to people who identify as homosexual. This is part of many people's personal experience, but is not an insight incorporated into the generally accepted notion of a homosexual minority in society; it is not the common-sense way of seeing things. This is not to say that the mental adjustments that make this possible[30] were in operation in the sixteenth and seventeenth centuries, but their existence today in the historian's own society should alert him or her to the possibility that such adjustments could have been operating in the earlier period being looked at. For the moment I ask no more than that it should be accepted as a working hypothesis that this was one of the means by which the conflict between individual desire and social values was being solved. What evidence is there?

It will inevitably be very difficult — although not impossible[31] — to directly illustrate a mechanism of this kind, as by its very nature it leaves few if any traces. And yet if we begin by looking for signs of its influence rather than for it in itself, it turns out to be a good deal easier to see at work than the more limited responses already discussed. If we are ready to recognise them, the signs have been manifest from the beginning. For when one looks at the circumstantial details of how homosexuality was conceived of and how it was expressed in concrete social forms, it becomes obvious how very easy it was in Renaissance England — far more so than today — for a cleavage of this kind to exist, between an individual's behaviour and his awareness of its significance.

Firstly the way homosexuality was conceived of: how possible was it to avoid identifying with the 'sodomite' who was the companion of witches and Papists, of werewolves and agents of the King of Spain?[32] When the world inhabited by the conventional image of the sodomite was so distant from everyday life, it cannot have been hard. In many cases this conclusion would have been reinforced by the disparity between the nature assigned to homosexuality as a force of anarchy and disorder, and the actual state of affairs, which was often very much at odds with this.[32] If one sets against these notions the existence of homosexuality institutionalised in the household[33] — orderly and hierarchical as it was — it becomes clear just how great the disparity was. It cannot have been difficult to avoid identifying the two. In such circumstances historians should be watchful for signs, however difficult to detect, that for someone involved in a homosexual relationship the nature of that relationship might not have been as obvious to him as it is to them.

There is an example of this actually at work in the case of Meredith Davy, which was mentioned in the last chapter in a different context.[34] The circumstances seem straightforward enough at first sight: a labourer hauled before the magistrates after sexually abusing the young apprentice with whom he shared a bed. On closer examination however they do not seem at all straightforward, at least in some respects. We shall need to come back to these in a moment, but there is one surprising circumstance among them which is very pertinent here. In view of the hatred and loathing with which homosexuality was habitually referred to, one naturally expects that Meredith Davy would have gone to great lengths to hide his sexual interest in the boy; not to have done so would surely have been wildly dangerous. It therefore comes as a considerable surprise to read it quietly mentioned in the depositions, almost in passing, that Davy was not alone with the boy when he was forcing his attentions on him: throughout the whole time this was happening there was a witness, a servant who slept in the same room with them, to whom the creaking of their bed and the groans and cries of the boy were quite audible as he later gave evidence; and this was repeated on Sunday and holiday nights for something like a month. This is so much at odds with what one would expect that it is difficult to believe Davy was seeing himself in the same light that we see him in, or that he thought that the intense hatred with which sodomites were spoken of was likely to be turned on him. It is perhaps this which best explains Davy's bewildered behaviour before the magistrate, simultaneously protesting his innocence and unable to answer the detailed evidence of the other servant and the boy himself: he 'denieth that he ever used any unclean action with the said boy as they lay in bed together; and more he sayeth not.' What more was there to say?

Images of homosexuality were not alone in effectively concealing homosexual behaviour. The same effect was produced by the social forms homosexual behaviour tended to take: the village community, the educational system, the theatres, the conventions of prostitution, and above all the influence of the household; none of these were distinctive of homosexuality.[35] Mediated as homosexuality then was by social relationships that did not take their form from homosexuality and were not exclusive to it, the barrier between heterosexual and homosexual behaviour (despite the impression contemporaries gave to the contrary) was in practice vague and imprecise. There was little or no reason for homosexual relations to influence people's lives outside the strictly sexual sphere. It is not then difficult to understand the instances one comes across of figures who combined a lively progress of homosexual adventures, possibly for many years, with an otherwise entirely conventional life.

One was the Rev. John Wilson of Arlington in Sussex, whose energetic sexual life has already been mentioned: he 'divers times attempted to commit buggery with Nathaniel Browne, Samuel Andrews and Robert Williams his parishioners...that (as he shamed not to profess) they might make up his number eighteen'.[36] Yet at the same time he was a conventionally married

man and a Laudian clergyman.[37] The sharp contradiction in his
life was by no means unique. Sir Anthony Ashley was a courtier at
the court of James I, also conventionally married and with a
daughter, yet was described by a contemporary as someone 'who
never loved any but boys'.[38] Similarly the emigrant to the
American colonies mentioned in Winthrop's *History of New
England* and referred to earlier was also married and yet began his
homosexual liaisons in England, continuing them with 'a great
part of the youth of Guilford' after arriving in the New World.[39]
A married Somerset innkeeper George Dowdeney was charged
before the magistrates in 1622 with a homosexual offence, but
only after having enjoyed a succession of homosexual encounters,
according to the evidence which only then surfaced, for at least
the previous fourteen years.[40]

Each of these illustrates in miniature the same point: outside an
immediately sexual context, there was little or no social pressure
for someone to define for himself what his sexuality was. And the
way homosexuality was conceived of and understood did not
encourage him to make that connection had he wished to, which
was unlikely. Given the intense hostility homosexuality aroused
when it was visible and its influence on a widely shared
mythology, it is difficult to believe that many would have tried to
overcome the effects of this hostility by scepticism and criticism:
and given the ease with which the individual could quietly avoid
recognising his sexual behaviour for what it was and thus avoid
the question altogether, it is possible to see how for many that
simple expedient was the solution.

But would they have been left in peace to pursue it? It hardly
seems likely when one reads the expressions of fear and
unrestrained hatred that come so easily to hand; when the
government and the Justices of the Peace were bent on
murderous persecution, and when one's neighbours would have
been sufficiently horrified as to have had no compunction
whatsoever in denouncing a sodomite. In such a hostile
atmosphere a merely individualistic solution, however subtle,
could not have survived had it had to face the full force of that
antagonism. The clearest measure of how far it had in practice to
do so is the records of the courts responsible for enforcing the
laws against buggery: the Assizes and from 1563 the Quarter
Sessions also; the ecclesiastical courts could also be involved to a

limited extent by way of complaint against someone's scandalous life, but as buggery was a felony it was not directly a matter for them. If one approaches the records of the courts which were involved fresh from the horrified condemnations of jurists and legal writers, one might understandably expect to find an army of martyrs. 'A detestable and abominable sin' wrote Edward Coke typically enough, 'it deserveth death.'[41] But whatever the legal theorists implied, the actual practice of the courts was not at all in line with this. Alan Macfarlane's search in the Essex Quarter Sessions records for 1556-1680 did not produce a single case concerned with homosexuality, and his search of the Essex Assize records for 1560-1680 produced only one (dated 1669).[42] A similar conclusion was the result of G.R. Quaife's study of the Somerset Quarter Sessions depositions for 1601-1660: the Somerset Justices took a lively interest in sexual immorality, but in all this period only two of the depositions involved homosexuality.[43] As for the Assizes, the rarity of indictments here is now being conclusively demonstrated by the monumental multi-volumed calendar of the Home Counties Assizes in the reigns of Elizabeth I and James I, being edited by Professor J.S. Cockburn. The Home Counties Assizes are crucial in this respect in that, although there are some gaps in their extant records, they are the only largely complete series covering a wide geographical area and a substantial period of time. And for the 66-year period 1559-1625, for the whole of the counties of Kent, Sussex, Hertfordshire and Essex there are only four indictments for sodomy.[44] The evidence of the courts, Assizes and Quarter Sessions alike, tends to the same conclusion: prosecutions for homosexuality were very rare occurrences, and the concern of the courts with the regulation of homosexual behaviour was only marginal.

That is a conclusion borne out by an analysis of the prosecutions that do occur, for they fall into a limited number of clearly recognisable classes. One of these are those which occur in times of social upheaval. A likely response to the suffering this brings is to seek a scapegoat, and in the mentality of seventeenth-century England a sodomite was a likely candidate for that role: it was exactly at such times that fear crystallised around those customary figures of evil which in more normal times were kept at a distance from everyday life, figures such as the trio of the Papist, the witch and the sodomite.[45] One victim of this seems to have been the Domingo Cassedon Drago mentioned in the last chapter, who was recorded as being in the Hampshire county gaol in 1647 awaiting return to Essex to face trial for 'a buggery' he was supposed to have committed.[46] His arrest came in the wake of just such a period of dislocation produced by the ravages of the Civil War, and coincided significantly with the presence of the witch-craze in Essex, in the person of Matthew Hopkins the witch-finder. What marked Drago out for such treatment? There is good reason to think that it was the colour of his skin. A member of a non-European race was more than a merely unusual sight in mid seventeenth-century England: he specifically brought to mind the image of the sodomite, which was linked in the literature of the time with non-European races.[47] Drago's homosexuality was all too likely to attract attention. The word 'negar' (negro) is used four times in the short entry in the Order Book concerning him. It is not surprising that he should have been singled out. A similar period of social upheaval surrounded the trial and execution of John Swan and John Litster for sodomy in Edinburgh in 1570. Their arrest coincided with the social tensions brought about by the coming of the Reformation to Scotland and the return of the Calvinist exiles; and as with Drago in 1647 it was accompanied by the arrival of the witch craze.[48] In each case similar pressures were at work; in times of social disturbance like these people are apt to see in the world about them the image of the figures they fear: a 'sodomite' in seventeenth-century England as much as a 'communist' or 'zionist' today.

But such times are rare, and when they have passed the archetypes of fear return to the imagination; most of the prosecutions for homosexuality were not of this kind. A second recognisable class of prosecutions consists of those where one suspects behind them a malicious intent. Since the thirteenth century a charge of homosexuality was a convenient one to bring against someone who could be charged with nothing else. Whether the trial and execution of John Atherton, bishop of Waterford and Lismoie, for sodomy in 1640 was more than a contrivance is open to doubt, but it was clearly a convenient means of destroying an appointee of the hated Strafford.[49] And the humble as well as the powerful could be victims of this. In 1615 a certain Edward Bawde, described variously as a 'yeoman' and a 'victualler', was indicted before the Middlesex Sessions of the Peace 'charged to have attempted to bugger one Henry Burnell.'[50] There is good reason to think that the prosecution was malicious. Edward Bawde was certainly an unpopular and contentious character and a likely victim for a malicious prosecution: he had already been prosecuted for selling ale and beer by defective measures;[51] and after the 1615 indictment had blown over he reappeared at the Sessions and was bound over to be of good behaviour on another charge.[52] He was the sort of man likely to make enemies. And the Henry Burnell mentioned in the charge had been in court himself on a charge of unlawful entry[53] and was hardly a reliable witness. The entry for Bawde in the Sessions Register for 1615 stands next to an entry for Henry Burnell and a certain Lewis Owen 'suspected to have conspired in a wrongful accusation against Edward Bawde',[54] which in the cirumstances was quite probable. An allegation of homosexuality whether true or not was a convenient means of carrying out a malicious design, against the humble and the powerful alike.[55]

But the most numerous class of prosecutions was those which were the result of an incident involving either a breach of the peace or a breach of social order. The most obvious instances of this are cases involving violence. Curtailing lawless violence was one of the principal objectives of the Justices; and — homosexuality apart — violence was always something likely to attract their attention. It did so in the case of Alban Cooke, a Hoxton yeoman who was accused of sexually assaulting a youth by the name of John Townsend and was tried at the Middlesex Sessions of the Peace in 1613.[56] It was also the principal element in the case of Meredith Davy.[57] We should link with these the kind of case one frequently comes across where a prosecution has been brought as a result of persistent complaints by an outraged parent; as much as the cases involving violence, what was offended against was the stability of the social order. Typical of such prosecutions was that of James Slater, a barber in Ware in Hertfordshire, who was tried for sodomy at the Hertford Assizes in 1607; the incident had involved the young son of one of his neighbours, and it is clear from the recognizances that the prosecution was brought as a result of the persistent efforts of the boy's father.[58] A similar prosecution was heard at the Middlesex Sessions in 1618 when a Frenchman, Peter de Guy, was tried for sodomy; the offence apparently involved the son of a local knight, and his influence appears as the driving force behind the prosecution.[59] This is also the reason why George Dowdeney, mentioned earlier, was eventually prosecuted for sodomy, after having enjoyed without trouble a series of homosexual encounters stretching over the previous fourteen years at least. These finally came to an end when he tried to force his attentions on the son of one of his neighbours. The father of the boy took strong exception to this and went to the Justices; and with the ensuing notoriety a good deal else then began to come out.[60]

In each of these instances what was at issue was primarily the maintenance of the social order, in particular the maintenance of parental rights, and only secondarily the enforcement of the legislation against homosexuality. So long as homosexuality was expressed through established social institutions, in normal times the courts were not concerned with it; and generally this meant patriarchal institutions — the household, the educational system, homosexual prostitution and the like.[61] Noticeably absent are prosecutions for homosexuality between masters and servants unless undue violence was involved or for offences involving homosexual prostitution, although the literary evidence shows how common homosexual prostitution was. In the same way the homosexual component in the educational system was largely unrecognised by the courts; and where, as we have seen, it was brought to their attention, it was not taken seriously.[62] Despite the contrary impression given by legal theorists, so long as homosexual activity did not disturb the peace or the social order, and in particular so long as it was consistent with patriarchal mores, it was largely in practice ignored. There was no systematic persecution, none of the periodic purges directed against homosexuality which were to be a feature of English society in the eighteenth century and later. In this respect England may have differed from continental Europe;[63] there are no parallels in England to the periodic peaks in persecution which occurred in Calvinistic Geneva[64] or to the mass panic witnessed by the traveller William Lithgow when he visited Malta in 1616:

> The fifth day of my staying here, I saw a Spanish soldier and a Maltese boy burnt in ashes, for the public profession of sodomy; and long or night there were above a hundred bardassos, whorish boys, that fled away to Sicily in a galliot for fear of fire...[65]

What we see in the English material are rather isolated

individuals who fell foul of the law in circumstances which were out of the ordinary, usually because their homosexual behaviour involved some breach of the peace: a yeoman farmer or a labourer who went too far in forcing his attentions on someone who was not interested, a man caught in his house with the son of a neighbour, an unpopular innkeeper, or a stranger in the neighbourhood. But these instances are representative of the working of the legal apparatus rather than the pattern of life in the everyday world. In general homosexual behaviour went largely unrecognised or ignored, both by those immediately involved and by the communities in which they lived;[66] in this the individual and society were at one. When a prosecution for sodomy was brought it must have been a bewildering and shattering experience, but it was a very rare one.

This was not tolerance. There is no justification whatsoever for not accepting at their face value the expressions of fear and loathing which are to be found so readily in the literature of the time; and they do not square with any notion of a *de facto* tolerance. Nor does such an explanation accord with the attitudes and behaviour of this society towards homosexuality outside of itself. Its readiness, even eagerness, to recognise homosexuality in an alien context is in marked contrast to its reluctance to do so within. Several travellers wrote detailed and horrified accounts of the homosexuality they witnessed in relatively more tolerant societies: William Lithgow on southern Europe and Moslem Turkey and North Africa;[67] Thomas Herbert on Persia and the Far East;[68] and George Turbervile, Elizabeth I's ambassador to Russia, on homosexuality among the Russian peasantry.[69] All three explicitly linked the homosexuality they encountered with the barbarous or Papistical nature of these societies, leaving the reader with the strong impression that in Protestant northern Europe such things were unknown. In this they were only retailing a common assumption. '*Le bougre Italien*' according to Thomas Browne was the national character of the Italians;[70] and it was the Lombards, or so at least claimed Edward Coke, who first brought homosexuality into the country.[71] Coke also solemnly reminded his readers that 'bugeria is an Italian word'.[72] And such figures were not only the stuff of travellers' tales; when the alien was a foreigner living in the midst of English society it was all too likely to see its own shadow in him, as Domingo Cassedon Drago and Peter de Guy were to discover. The general indifference of English courts to homosexuality is not to be explained by any simple notion of a day-to-day tolerance.

It was not tolerance; it was rather a reluctance to recognise homosexual behaviour, a sluggishness in accepting that what was being seen was indeed the fearful sin of sodomy. It was this that made it possible for the individual to avoid the psychological problems of a homosexual relationship or a homosexual encounter, by keeping the experience merely casual and undefined: readily expressed and widely shared though the prevalent attitude to homosexuality was, it was kept at a distance from the great bulk of homosexual behaviour by an unwillingness to link the two. Inevitably the evidence for a mechanism of this kind, although in this case very strong, is largely indirect: the traces it leaves are in significant discrepancies at the points where one would expect to see the influence of hostility. This is largely the case here, but not wholly so; at times it is possible to see the mechanism at work. There is an example of it in the evidence of one of the witnesses in the prosecution of George Dowdeney mentioned earlier. The witness told the Justice of an incident which had occurred some fourteen years earlier when Dowdeney had forced his attentions on him. His explanation as to why he had not mentioned this before might well strike us as rather odd:

> ...he spake not thereof unto anyone ever since until about a week last past, and thinks he should never have spoken thereof, but that now of late he heard diverse others charge him with facts of the like kind.[73]

This it should be noted is not a confession, and in the circumstances he could quite reasonably have explained his silence as the result of feeling intimidated. It is an explanation, and one it was expected the Justice would regard as reasonable. Is he saying that it was only when he heard other 'facts of the like kind' that he realised the seriousness of this and that he had a duty to bring it to the attention of the Justices? If so, it is just the kind of reaction which the broader circumstances we have seen would lead us to expect. There are several examples of the same thing in Meredith Davy's case. Davy's own apparent failure to recognise that his behaviour could be treated so seriously has already been noted; but this is by no means the end of the surprises the depositions in this case hold for the researcher. Davy was not alone in his reluctance to recognise his behaviour for what it manifestly was; it appears to have been shared by virtually everyone else involved. For example there is the behaviour of Richard Bryant, the servant who slept in the room with Davy and the boy and who was the chief impetus behind the prosecution. He eventually took the matter to the mistress of the household,[74] but it is striking as one reads his evidence how long it took him to realise what was going on and how reluctant he is likely to appear to us now to have been to draw the obvious conclusions:

> ...several times within this month last past as he hath layn in the same chamber in another bed where the said Meredith and the said John lay together, he hath heard the said John groan and cry out, not knowing the reason thereof; and hath heard the bed wherein they lay crack, which after he had heard several times he began to suspect what the reason thereof should be...[75]

But what is really astonishing is the reaction of the household when Bryant did go to the mistress and the boy told all. Everything this society had to say about the nature of homosexuality and its horror would naturally lead us to expect a horrified reaction; at the very least one expects that Davy would have been locked up. The Justices' casual conclusion to the boy's evidence therefore comes with a jolt: 'since which time he hath layn quietly with him.'[76] Not only was he not locked up: he was not even removed from the boy's bed. This is not the behaviour of people who think they are dealing with a monster in human form. Both of these cases illustrate in microcosm the discrepancy between this society's extreme hostility to homosexuality which one comes across when homosexuality was being referred to in the abstract and its reluctance to recognise it in most concrete situations.

The discrepancy is so great as to demand an explanation. It lies in part in the influences already seen at work on the level of the individual. Was society any more likely than the individual to recognise in the everyday reality of homosexuality the figure of the sodomite when this figure was spoken of in imagery so divorced from the social forms homosexuality actually took? Perhaps in times of social upheaval the desperate and the disturbed might see the world in such apocalyptic terms, but for the far greater part of the time the answer is surely: no. And when homosexuality had no distinctive social characteristics of its own beyond the immediately sexual, on whatever scale it was viewed its visibility would be curtailed.[77] There is though a possible major difference here between the individual and society: the individual certainly had a motive for avoiding a clear definition of his aberrant sexual behaviour. Was there then also some benefit in this for society as a whole? Indeed there was.

The explanation is partly in the late age of first marriage.[78] From about the fifteenth century the normal age for a man to marry for the first time was in his late twenties or early thirties; this was true of western European society in general. His marriage would normally coincide with him setting up his own household, with the period before marriage commonly having been passed in his father's household or as a servant in someone's else's while he (and his future bride) accumulated the capital they needed. This long period of waiting had considerable economic advantages. Firstly it was an indirect form of birth control and operated to keep the population in line with economic resources. And secondly there were the obvious advantages to the economy that capital accumulation brought. It was then a social regulator of considerable importance; but it carried with it certain social problems, the most obvious of which was the long period of time after puberty when a young man was under considerable pressure to avoid potentially procreative sexual intercourse. There had to be alternatives; and one of these was homosexuality. Of course it was only one among several, and it would have been quite out of character for this society to countenance any conscious tolerance; but it does mean that if there were mechanisms in existence which, while leaving the taboo against homosexuality itself intact, could nevertheless quietly keep homosexuality as something casual, undefined and largely unrecognised, then these mechanisms would have a stabilising influence to the general benefit. It was in society's interest, as much as the individual's, to leave such mechanisms alone.

But although this certainly was a factor in the process at work, it does not wholly account for it. There is for example no evidence to suggest that homosexuality was treated differently as between married and unmarried persons; that would be a surprising absence if this were all that was involved. Also the late age of marriage was not confined to the sixteenth and seventeenth centuries: it was still present as late as the early decades of the twentieth century, by which time the social configuration of homosexuality had changed profoundly. This does not mean that we cannot see it as part of the context of English society in the sixteenth and seventeenth centuries, where it was a factor at work in encouraging a minimal level of recognition of homosexuality; but it cannot have been the only one.

A deeper need was being met also. There was a fundamental incompatibility between English society's uncompromising rejection of homosexuality and the hard and stony facts it somehow had to come to terms with. At the point at which this book begins, around the year 1550, its attitude was already fixed. It was an inheritance of the late Middle Ages, a product of the rigidity and contracting horizons of the Europe of the thirteenth century, part of its retreat from the expansive culture of the eleventh and early twelfth centuries.[79] Hostility to homosexuality, unlike many other legacies of the late Middle Ages, showed no signs of atrophy: it had all the robust vitality of a living idea, and it had long been built into its dominant intellectual traditions. This rejection was total and unbending; there was no civilisation in the world at that time with as violent an antipathy to homosexuality as that of western Europe.[80] And yet it was faced with the unalterable fact that homosexuality did exist within it on a massive and ineradicable scale. Writ large, it was the same problem as faced the individual trying to reconcile the general hostility to homosexuality, which he could not help but in some degree share, with his own insistent sexual desires. And the solution was essentially the same for each of them: to keep the contact between the myths and symbols of homosexuality and homosexuality itself to a minimum, and to leave homosexual behaviour to be perceived and understood largely in different terms; to keep the two apart.

There is no need to seek a primary element in this. The individual solution and the social conditions and habits of mind that made it possible were two sides of the same thing; each equally required the other. The benefits they brought were not exclusively cause or effect; they were part of a coherent whole. The impression one is ultimately therefore left with is of something stable and unchanging. Homosexuality had a potentially disruptive effect, but it was held in check and successfully resolved. Hated and feared yet by the same token largely unrecognised and unformed, it remained ubiquitous potentially or actually within the architecture of society. This is why it is difficult to detect forms of homosexual behaviour which are distinctive of particular areas or social groups;[81] it was, quite simply, not socialised to any significant degree at all, for reasons which were important both to the individual and the community. The means by which this was achieved was a process of continuous adaptation, sometimes disastrous but largely nominal — a question of giving or withholding a name — as each accomodated itself to the facts. In detail it is a process, but viewed in its entirety the result is immobile, resolved and unchanging. And indeed if one looks at the place homosexuality occupied in English society during the century and a half from the close of the Middle Ages to the mid 1600s, there is little discernible change and little sign that there ever would be. Yet nothing could be more misleading. If we move only fifty years ahead, to the close of the seventeenth century, the picture is radically different. The habits of mind, the social structures and mechanisms that seemed to comprise so stable a whole have gone, and the historian is left with the uncanny feeling that he or she is far more aware of what they had been than the people then living. In only two or three generations they have become history; and what has replaced them, which is now what must be described, is brilliantly different.

Chapter Four:

Molly[1]

Holborn's gleaming office blocks and noisy traffic suggest little beyond the commerce which is the life of this part of London; but if you walk down Charterhouse Street, one of Holborn's main roads, you will see on your left a flight of steps and at their feet, incongruous among the twentieth-century bustle, a quiet and narrow cobbled street. This is Saffron Hill,[2] and it remains today much what it was two and a half centuries ago. Saffron Hill is one of those parts of Holborn that have somehow avoided redevelopment, and you can still walk down its whole length until what was once its southern extension is lost under the road and the office blocks across the way. But had you walked down Saffron Hill at the beginning of the eighteenth century, you would have been able to continue your journey south into Field Lane, as a certain Samuel Stevens did one dark Sunday evening in November 1725. Field Lane was even narrower than Saffron Hill, part of the warren of insanitary courts and dark alleys that stretched east of Smithfield Market towards the City, hopelessly overcrowded since the exodus beyond the City boundaries that followed the Great Fire of 1666. It was an easy place to become lost in, but Samuel Stevens knew quite where he was going. He was looking for a certain house: the house of Margaret Clap.

When 'I went to the prisoner's house in Field Lane,' he said at her trial eight months later, 'I found between 40 and 50 men making love to one another, as they called it. Sometimes they would sit in one another's laps, kissing in a lewd manner and using their hands indecently. Then they would get up, dance and make curtsies, and mimic the voices of women... Then they would hug, and play, and toy, and go out by couples into another room on the same floor to be married, as they called it.'[3]

Samuel Stevens was probably an agent for the Societies for the Reformation of Manners, a crusading religious organisation which played an important role in prosecuting sodomites, prostitutes and sabbath-breakers.[4] His visit that Sunday in November 1725 was not to be his last; he returned, taking notes, on subsequent Sunday evenings, until the house and several others like it were raided in February 1726. The house in Field Lane was probably the largest of these houses in the London of the time. On a Sunday, which was its busiest night, it might have as many as fifty customers; and it was large enough for some of them to live there as lodgers. But it was only one of several; there was across London a network of such houses, known to society at large as well as their customers as 'molly houses' (or more rarely 'mollying culls').[5] They were essentially very similar; during the trials that followed the raids of February 1726 they were described in the evidence given in much the same terms as those used by Samuel Stevens in describing Margaret Clap's house. An agent who visited one of these, a molly house in the City, explained to the court at the trial of its proprietor what he encountered when he arrived:

> On Wednesday the 17th of November last I went to the prisoner's house in Beech Lane, and there I found a company of men fiddling and dancing and singing bawdy songs, kissing and using their hands in a very unseemly manner... In a large room there we found one a-fiddling and eight more a-dancing country dances... Then they sat in one another's lap, talked bawdy, and practiced a great many indecencies. There was a door in the great room, which opened into a little room, where there was a bed, and into this little room several of the company went...[6]

Unlike this one, some of the molly houses were in private rooms in a tavern rather than in a house such as Margaret Clap's; while others were private houses that had become established as open meeting-places for 'mollies', as sodomites were popularly known by the first decade of the eighteenth century. At least they were sufficiently open for a stranger to be able to arrive and be admitted, as Samuel Stevens was, much as he might have been at a tavern. But whether the molly house was a private house or part of a tavern it fitted a pattern. For example there was usually

From *The Women-Hater's Lamentation*, an anti-homosexual broadsheet published in 1707.

drinking. If the molly house was not in a tavern, the owner of the house brought drink in for customers and sold it there. The drinking went together with singing and dancing and the drunken good humour one would expect. It was also possible for a visitor to have sexual intercourse in the house itself: for many a molly house would have been the only place where this was possible with any safety. Contemporary descriptions either in evidence before the courts or in the popular journalism the cases gave rise to make much of this; they inevitably concentrated on the sensational aspects of the molly houses, such as the alleged sexual debauchery. But this gives a misleading impression. Sex was the root of the matter, but it was as likely to be expressed in drinking together, in flirting and gossip and in a circle of friends as in actual liaisons. Surrounded as the molly houses were by intense disapproval and at least partly hidden, they must have seemed like any ghetto, at times claustrophobic and oppressive, at others warm and reassuring. It was a place to take off the mask. It is as much in such terms as in actual sexual encounters that we should now envisage what a molly house was like.

The molly houses were scattered across the whole of the built-up area north of the Thames, which by the early eighteenth century stretched without interruption from the slums of Wapping through the City and the environs of Smithfield Market to the wealthy western suburbs before the countryside began again beyond Westminster. To the east of Margaret Clap's house there was the molly house in Beech Lane whose description has already been quoted, in the heart of the City itself. Within walking distance of Field Lane, at the top of the Old Bailey and near one of the main thoroughfares into the City there was a molly house in the shadow of Newgate prison and the Sessions House, where the trials after the catastrophe of 1726 were to be held. Further west in a quiet court in what is now Soho, then a fashionable residential area, there was a molly house in some private rooms in a tavern named the Red Lion. And there were several others nearby, one a brandy shop in Charing Cross[7] and a second amidst the bustle and life of Drury Lane. Further west still there was a molly house in a back room provided by the landlord of the Royal Oak, a tavern at the corner of the magnificent St James's Square looking onto the splendours of Pall Mall and St James's Park. And across the park, at its south side, was an area of the park which was one of several public places where it was possible to make casual homosexual contacts; the same function was served by the piazzas of Covent Garden, the latrines at Lincoln's Inn, and the walk by the south side of the wall that divided the upper and middle Moorfields (a grassy open space in the City).[8]

Such places, together with the molly houses, merged into a coherent social milieu. It is perhaps difficult to imagine someone from the slums of the east end of London appearing at the Royal Oak in St James's Square, but there was considerable movement between the molly houses, as we can see in a description one of the investigators later gave of how an informer had taken him on a tour of several of the molly houses while he had been gathering information before the raids.[8a] The molly houses and the casual meeting-places such as St James's Park were not separate entities but were part of a specifically homosexual world, a society within a society. The molly houses of the early eighteenth century are in sharp contrast to the socially amorphous forms homosexuality had taken a century earlier; Elizabethan or Jacobean England had no parallel to the separate world it represented. This was not primarily though that there now existed taverns, or something like taverns, and parks and public squares with a reputation for homosexuality. For example, St James's Park had been a source of casual homosexual liasons for more than half a century at least.[9] And if the suggestion made in the last chapter is correct, that the homosexual brothels of early and mid seventeenth-century London were more like taverns than brothels in the strict sense of the term, then it is possible to detect a line of continuity between the homosexual 'brothels' of the seventeenth century and the molly houses of the eighteenth. This is particularly likely in that prostitution, while an important part of homosexual life in seventeenth-century London (and again in the nineteenth century), was only marginally significant in the eighteenth century. With the element of prostitution removed, a homosexual 'brothel' in Elizabethan Southwark would have been very like a molly house in eighteenth-century Holborn. The difference was not primarily in the molly houses themselves or in the mere existence of places such as St James's Park: it lay rather in what they amounted to within society, in the part they played.

Firstly, the milieu of the molly houses existed in its own right independently of the individuals who might compose it at any one time, as one can see for example in the married men who entered and left it over and again, apparently living double lives;[10] for them it was an objective fact. Similarly, it cut across social classes and was composed of individuals drawn from the whole spectrum of the lower and lower-middle classes: references to a 'chairman',[11] i.e. one of the two men who carried a sedan chair, or a 'man of good business . . . [who] was fallen into poverty',[12] jostle in the accounts of the trials with references to the under City marshall[13] or a wealthy tavern-keeper and landlord.[14] The society of the molly houses did not follow class lines but rather tended to dissolve them. It did so because it was not mediated by existing social forms, of class or otherwise: it was set alongside them, a social institution in its own right. But most of all what gave it its independence in society was its elaboration of its own distinctive conventions: ways of dressing, of talking, distinctive gestures and distinctive acts with an understood meaning, its own jargon. It was out of such things, mentioned in the accounts quoted earlier, that its particular identity was made, and it was they that distinguished its culture from that of society at large. In part these had an immediate practical benefit: some were signs by which mollies were unobtrusively able to identify each other. Others were more oblique: they were a language tailored to fit the experiences and characteristics of the sexual life of a molly house. In origin they were usually heterosexual terms turned to new and ironic applications. The room in a molly house where couples were able to have sexual relations was the 'chapel', and the act itself 'marrying' or a 'wedding night'; similarly a 'husband' was a sexual partner. One gets the impression, however, as one comes across these terms in the trials, that expressions such as these had become so familiar as to have lost their ironic edge; they had become part of the common coinage because they were about what was unique in the life of the molly houses.

That way of life was the product of a complex tissue of customs and conventions, but the one element in them that most scandalised contemporary journalists writing about the molly houses was the extravagant effeminacy and transvestism they could involve; and this was at the root of the way they worked. Ned Ward's claim that 'they rather fancy themselves women, imitating all the little vanities that custom has reconciled to the female sex, affecting to speak, walk, tattle, curtsy, cry, scold, and to mimic all manner of effeminacy that ever has fallen within their several observations'[15] is remarkably close to first-hand descriptions of the molly houses, such as that of a drag ball at the molly house in the Old Bailey:

> ...they had no sooner entered but the Marshall was complemented by the company with the titles of Madam and Ladyship. The man asking the occasion of these uncommon devoirs, the Marshall said it was a familiar language peculiar to the house. The man was not long there before he was more surprised than at first. The men calling one another 'my dear' and hugging, kissing, and tickling each other as if they were a mixture of wanton males and females, and assuming effeminate voices and airs; some telling others that they ought to be whipped for not coming to school more frequently... Some were completely rigged in gowns, petticoats, headcloths, fine laced shoes, furbelowed scarves, and masks; some had riding hoods; some were dressed like milkmaids, others like shepherdesses with green hats, waistcoats, and petticoats; and others had their faces patched and painted and wore very extensive hoop petticoats, which had been very lately introduced.[16]

Transvestism of this kind had a function crucially different from that of Elizabethan or Jacobean London. Transvestism itself was not new, as one can see from the extensive contemporary description of it in Thomas Middleton's *Micro-Cynicon* published in 1599;[17] but the significance given to it a century later was radically different. In Middleton's book the narrator's sorry tale began, he tells us, when one day he saw in the street what he took to be an extraordinarily beautiful woman and fell in love with her. The woman was in fact a man and a transvestite, a 'painted puppet' 'in a nymph's attire'. However the narrator is at first unaware of this, and all goes well — 'fair words I had, for store of coin I gave' — until his passion proves too much to be resisted: the attempt is made, and his mistake is revealed. Middleton's book is largely taken up with his complaints of how he has been duped in this; but it is also very revealing for the social historian, for the transvestite is presented as by no means an unusual figure. Indeed Middleton claims:

> The streets are full of juggling parasites
> With the true shape of virgins' counterfeits.

Transvestism was as common in Elizabethan London as it was to be a century later, but there are sharp differences between transvestism in the two periods; and one of them is present in Middleton's reference to the streets as the haunt of transvestites. Transvestism in the eighteenth-century molly houses was something that took place behind closed doors: it had nothing to do with the streets. The transvestism Thomas Middleton is describing was intended to deceive: that of an eighteenth-century molly house was not; it was quite obviously a man dressed in women's clothes. What then was its purpose? The answer is in the other major difference between Middleton's tale and the conditions of the eighteenth century: Middleton's tale is not concerned with homosexuality. The whole point of the story is that the transvestite was trying to avoid sexual intercourse so as to avoid being discovered. His motives were apparently mercenary, leading to the suggestion — which is probably the best explanation of the sexual ambiguity of the story — that Middleton looked on transvestism as a vice in its own right. The transvestism of the eighteenth-century molly house was in this respect the very opposite. It was about homosexuality; it was not intended to deceive and, as the molly houses themselves, was wisely kept as unobtrusive as possible. Effeminacy and transvestism with specifically homosexual connotations were a crucial part of what gave the molly houses their identity.

The molly houses were not of course isolated from the rest of society. Homosexuality in this form was hardly less subject to broader social influences than the more diffuse homosexuality of early seventeenth-century society. The use of terms such as 'chapel' or 'wedding night', for example, although their meanings may have been radically revised to meet new needs, show how strong these broader influences were even in the case of the molly houses; transvestism is an even clearer illustration of this. Nor should we suppose that the more socially diffuse homosexuality of the earlier period ceased to exist, especially in rural areas; it is scarcely possible for example to imagine a network of molly houses existing outside a large city. There is no reason to suppose that the traditional forms did not continue. It is rather there was now a tension that had not existed before. Alongside the old forms of society in which homosexuality had appeared, new meanings were now being attached to homosexuality: it was more than a mere sexual act. The new forms may even have involved only a minority of homosexual acts, but they overshadowed the old: they were a radical extension of the meaning of homosexuality, and they were far more brilliant.[18]

It is not therefore surprising that they attracted to themselves persecution on a scale and of an immediacy unknown before. More than forty people were arrested in one night when the molly house in Field Lane was broken up. And the people in Margaret Clap's house were not the only ones to be caught in the trap; at or around the same time similar raids were made on molly houses across London. In all something like twenty molly houses were broken up around this time.[19] Clearly it was a thorough and carefully planned operation which must have been in preparation for several months. This was without parallel before the closing years of the seventeenth century.

At the trials in 1726 it was said that investigators such as Samuel Stevens first became aware of the molly houses through an informer, a mysterious figure referred to merely as 'P':

> The discovery of the molly houses was chiefly owing to a quarrel betwixt P_____ and _____ Harrington; for upon this quarrel P_____, to be revenged on Harrington, had blabbed something of the secret and afterwards gave a large information. The mollies had heard a little of the first discovery but did not imagine how far he had proceeded and what further designs he had upon them.[20]

As we shall see, the idea that the molly houses were 'discovered' is a naive view of what happened; certainly though the raids were a long time in the making, and extensive — and as events proved effective — preparations were made. One might well wonder who was making these preparations, for they were most unlikely to have been the handiwork of the parish constables, the only police force London had at the time, aptly described by a modern historian as 'at best illiterate fools, and at worst as corrupt as the criminal classes from which not a few sprang'.[21] The one organisation which was clearly both able and willing to mount an exercise of this kind was the Societies for the Reformation of Manners, which we have already met in the person of Samuel Stevens, probably one of their agents. The declared purpose of the Societies was to lay information before the magistrates against sabbath-breakers, drunkenness and debauchery. The concern with debauchery apparently extended to homosexuality: an account of the Societies' work published in 1738 and covering the previous 44 years credits it with instigating the prosecution of numerous sodomites and sodomitical houses.[22] There is little doubt that behind the trials of 1726 we can see the all-too-effective activity of the Societies for the Reformation of Manners.

The first batch of trials took place in April. Those arrested included Gabriel Lawrence and William Griffin, a milkman and an upholsterer; both had been visitors at Margaret Clap's house, and William Griffin had also been a lodger there for several years. A third prisoner, George Kedger, had been a visitor at the Red Lion in Soho mentioned earlier. With these were the trials of two others who had themselves kept molly houses: Thomas Wright the proprietor of the molly house in Beech Lane and George Whitle that of the molly house at the Royal Oak in St James's Square. At least one of the others arrested had already died in prison; several others had managed to escape, either by leaving London altogether or by keeping hidden. The evidence at the trials rested partly on that of the constables and the agents of the Societies for the Reformation of Manners who had visited the molly houses before the raids, but principally on two young men who were crucial to what now happened.

One was Thomas Newton, 'a very pretty fellow' who had been closely connected with Margaret Clap's house and was probably a prostitute. The other was the sinister figure of Ned Courtney, who although only eighteen at the time of the trials had already been in prison several times; Ned Courtney was undoubtedly a prostitute and probably also a petty criminal. He seems to have been a particularly vicious and ruthless character: George Kedger, when he was giving evidence, recalled the time when Ned Courtney had said to him that 'he wanted money, and money he would have by hook or by crook'. Presumably he got his money. He also got blood. On Monday, 9 May 1726 Gabriel Lawrence, William Griffin and Thomas Wright were hanged at Tyburn. George Kedger and George Whitle managed to escape this: George Kedger had also been found guilty but was reprieved; George Whitle had been acquitted after producing a crowd of witnesses to the effect that nothing untoward had been going on at the Royal Oak and that Ned Courtney, on whom most of the prosecution evidence rested, had quarrelled with him and was not to be trusted. The executions in May 1726 were not the end of the persecutions however. There was a second batch of trials the following July. Two of these arose out of the raids of 1726 but had probably been postponed while further evidence was collected; these included Margaret Clap's own trial. The others were probably the result of the furore which had been generated. Certainly in the months following the trials the authorities set out to trap mollies in places such as St James's Park; one of the prisoners tried in July 1726 had been arrested in such circumstances. After this second batch of trials the pressure on what remained of the molly houses and their culture greatly lessened, and there were few arrests in the years immediately following. For a time, the storm was over.

The raids and trials of 1726 were not the first time that pogroms of this kind had taken place: by the end of the seventeenth century they had already become a recurrent feature in and around London of society's reaction to homosexuality. In 1699 and again in 1707 there had already been pogroms of a similar nature, albeit on a smaller scale.

'There is at this time,' wrote a pamphleteer in 1699 in an anti-homosexual diatribe, 'several taken up at Windsor and others of the same gang now committed to Newgate, who were engaged in a more than beast-like confederacy among themselves for exercising this unnatural offence.'[23] The reference is somewhat obscure but clearly involved events which on a smaller scale were similar to those of 1725-26. Eight years later a similar sequence of events reoccurred, although as with those of 1699 there are problems in reconstructing them.[24] It is difficult to see what scale they were on: a broadsheet published at the time and a contemporary satirical poem describing the events differ both as regards the number of people involved and the number of those who died as a result of what happened. But certainly the events were on a sufficiently large scale as to make them a *cause célèbre* for several years to come, and at least three of those accused took their own lives rather than face the horrors of Tyburn and the violent hostility of the mob. Two of these can be named with some certainty: one was Mr Grant, a woollen draper; the other a Mr Jermain, 'late clerk of St Dunstan's in the East'. There is no reason to think that what happened in 1699, again in 1707 and once again in 1726 were the only attempts around this time to suppress the homosexual culture of the molly houses:[25] there may

well have been others also, and that of 1699 need not have been
the first. Yet as a social phenomenon they were something new;
they are in marked contrast to the circumstances that prevailed in
England up to the last quarter of the seventeenth century. Mass
arrests of this kind, of whole groups of people (or as many as
could be found), are not something we see in England before this
period. Up to the closing years of the seventeenth century
prosecutions for buggery were nearly always of isolated
individuals and never of groups of people, and when they do occur
they appear in a limited number of identifiable circumstances.
Something fundamental has changed that needs to be looked at
more closely.

It is not that homosexuality was more fiercely disapproved of.
There is no evidence whatsoever of any absolute increase in
hostility to homosexuality.[26] The vitriolic condemnations of it to
be read in sixteenth- and seventeenth-century literature are not
one whit less vicious than those of the following century: indeed
it is difficult to see how those of the eighteenth century could be
any more violent. The change is not absolute but rather in the
extent to which people actually came up against that hostility;
and the reason for the change is not in the hostility but in its
object. There was now a continuing culture to be fixed on and an
extension of the area in which homosexuality could be expressed
and therefore recognised; clothes, gestures, language, particular
buildings and particular public places — all could be identified as
having specifically homosexual connotations. In contrast, the
socially diffused homosexuality of the early seventeenth century
was far less obtrusive, and violent condemnations of it rarely had
any significance outside of a world of symbol and myth. The
unrestrained nature of the one and the unobtrusiveness of the
other were connected. Its successor in the world of the molly
houses was something that could easily be seen, and it was this
that brought upon it the persecution which for so long had been
often no more than an unrealised potential. Its visibility was its
bane.

If the existence of a homosexual subculture gave hostility to
homosexuality an object on which it could now fasten, then it
could no longer be easily ignored. A servant in a Jacobean
household, or an Elizabethan schoolmaster, who lived in
circumstances in which homosexuality had a quietly institutionalised place, might well not think of homosexual behaviour in

terms as awesome as those of the anarchic 'sodomite':
homosexuality's limited social implications and the exotic terms
in which 'sodomy' was conceived of made an evasion of this kind
relatively easy, and there were powerful motives why society
should leave it undisturbed. But could that still hold in the
London of the Societies for the Reformation of Manners? This
would have been very difficult. It is not that most or even many
sodomites fell victim to the periodic outbursts. These were likely
to affect only those who were found in a molly house when it was
raided or were identified by an informer; and even then they
might be able to escape:

> ...one Peter Bavidge, who is not yet taken...[27]
>
> ...Thomas Phillips, who is since absconded...[28]

are unsurprising comments from the evidence given in the trials
of 1726. Considering the relatively small number of people who
were accused and tried that year, a great many more must have
stayed out of the way; certainly in 1707 the three or four arrests
we know of were matched by the many — one source estimated it
at one hundred[29] — who escaped or avoided detection. And the
violent suppression of the molly houses was itself only
intermittent. In each case the periodic persecutions were
followed by several years of relative calm. Someone who was a
molly might well, probably would, avoid arrest and the horrors
that followed, but what he could not avoid was the constant
possibility of this fate. And the implication of that? He could not
avoid knowing — he could not afford to avoid knowing — what
he was and what he was part of. He belonged to a culture that,
whatever the experiences of the individuals who composed it at
any given point, had suffered and survived periodic attempts to
exterminate it; and when such times came, what we see are arrests
en masse, not the isolated and bewildered individuals to be met
with in the legal records of a century before. There was then little
room for the quiet social and nominal adjustments of Elizabethan
and Jacobean society: there was a sharp and painful choice to be
made. It could still of course be avoided altogether, but now only
at the price of a continuing confusion of identity, which increased
in importance as the individual succeeded in making homosexual
contacts, inevitably in exposed and dangerous circumstances.

From *The Women-Hater's Lamentation* of 1707. The illustrations on this and the facing page are of suicides of mollies caught up in the pogrom of that year.

We can see an example of this at work in the evidence given in the case of a certain George Duffus, who was tried for sodomy in December 1721.[30] George Duffus was apparently not connected with the molly houses. His devout religious beliefs may have had something to do with this, but in any case his sexual contacts usually began by his engaging young men in religious conversation at the dissenting meeting-houses he visited. The conversation was no doubt genuine, but was also intended to be a prelude to an invitation, either then or at a similar later meeting, to return with them to their homes. After talking late into the night an invitation to stay until the following day would naturally follow. This would probably mean sharing a bed, and Duffus then took advantage of his opportunity. This was hardly a coherent and stable way of life, as much in his own image of himself as in the practical problems involved. Apart from the obvious dangers in making sexual contacts by such means, far more than were involved in visiting a molly house, something of George Duffus's mental anguish is apparent in the way he acted when he was arrested:

> He cried for mercy and begged that we would not expose him to public shame, adding that we were all sinners and it was hard for a man to suffer for the first fault.[31]

George Duffus's wretchedness is an indication of the price he had to pay for the unresolved tensions within him. A century before he might have been able to live this kind of life without its significance being fully apparent to him, and without the dangers and ordeal he eventually had to face; but in London in the 1720s this could not be.

The social context to George Duffus's dilemma was the violent immediacy that antagonism to homosexuality had now acquired; but there was a possible solution, or a partial one, had he been willing to take it. Paradoxically, it lay in the same circumstances that had given rise to these pressures in the first place: the existence of the molly houses themselves. If it was these that attracted attention and let the demons loose, it was also they that provided a shelter against them. On the simplest level the molly houses offered a relatively safe way of making sexual contacts, far safer than engaging someone in conversation at a dissenting meeting-house, or at work or in the streets. But they also offered something more. Firstly, sexual contacts or not, you were no longer alone. And this meant more than friendship, although no doubt that was important; what it gave the individual was the support of an aggressive and resilient culture. 'They . . . swore they would massacre anybody that should betray them'[32] was the response of one molly house to the possibility that they were indeed in danger. These were not idle words. When a molly house in Covent Garden was broken up in 1725, the crowded household, many of them in drag, met the raid with determined and violent resistance.[33] There were also other, less immediately dramatic, ways in which the mollies could defend themselves. There is, for example, evidence that some took the dangerous course of perjuring themselves to help mollies who had been arrested and were on trial. Such at least is the implication of Samuel Stevens's evidence at Margaret Clap's trial; he recounted how the company on one of his visits included a certain

> Derwin, who had been carried before Sir George Mertins for sodomitical practices with a linkboy. Derwin bragged how he had baffled the linkboy's evidence; and the prisoner at the same time boasted that what she had sworn before Sir George on Derwin's behalf was a great means of bringing him off.[34]

It is possible that a good many of the character witnesses who gave evidence at the sodomy trials of the accused's unimpeachable sexual morality were of this kind:

> The prisoner, in his defence, called some witnesses who had been his bedfellows. They deposed that he never offered any indecencies to them and that he had a wife and child and took care of his family.[35]

> I have been with him at the Oxfordshire Feast, where we have both got drunk and then come home together in a coach, and yet he never offered any such indecencies to me.[36]

> I believe he loved a girl too well to be concerned in other affairs.[37]

Witnesses of this kind could well be used to good effect, as they were in the trial of George Whitle. But above all the support the molly houses gave was in their culture, rather than in the rare instances when a witness with strong nerves and a credible tale was needed, or when it was possible to see off an agent of the

Societies for the Reformation of Manners. The most pressing problem was not physical persecution; in the end only a minority had to face that. It was rather in the confusion and guilt that had to be faced in the conflict between homosexual desire and the manifest disapproval of the world about the frightened individual. In providing a society in which homosexuality was normalised the molly houses lifted much of that burden. The world as seen through the eyes of someone accustomed to their society was very different from the view of it that prevailed elsewhere. There is a remarkable illustration of this in the evidence given at the trial of a certain Captain Rigby, who was charged in 1698 with attempted buggery.[38] Captain Rigby's trial was the result of his approach to a young man in St James's Park, by the name of William Minton, and their arrangement to meet a couple of days later. Rigby either made a mistake in taking Minton's measure, or Minton changed his mind: he went to his master, and he to the Justice of the Peace, and the meeting turned out to be a trap. However before the trap was sprung the waiting constables listened to Rigby talking to Minton about homosexuality:

> 'How can that be?' says Minton. 'I'll show you' says Rigby, 'for it is no more than was done in our forefathers' time;' and then to incite Minton thereto spake blasphemous words and further said that the French King did it and the Czar of Muscovy made Alexander, a carpenter, a prince for that purpose and affirmed he had seen the Czar of Muscovy through a hole at sea lie with Prince Alexander.[39]

The historian of homosexuality would dearly like to know what it was Captain Rigby said about 'our forefathers' time', but clearly this together with the remarks concerning the Russian and French monarchs functioned as a myth in which homosexuality was given a validation quite at odds with that given by society at large. But it was not only in myth that the molly houses served to normalise homosexuality. Above all this was achieved by means of their own society, both in the sense that within them homosexuality was no longer perverse as it was elsewhere, but also in that homosexuality quite objectively was the organising point around which its whole culture — its way of life, its manners, its behaviour — was built; within molly houses it was given a significance in direct proportion to its rejection elsewhere. And on the level of the individual that manifested itself as an identity, constructed around the fact of homosexuality but going far beyond it, an identity as a molly. The extent to which the identity was actually adopted would of course vary immensely. It is obviously not possible to build the whole of one's identity around the fact of homosexuality alone, or any other single fact; and indeed an individual can have several different sexual 'identities' at the same time, existing in tension with each other. There would inevitably be considerable differences, too, between an occasional visitor to a molly house, for example, and someone such as William Griffin who for nearly two years had been a lodger at Margaret Clap's. The identity existed rather as a possible lifestyle that integrated homosexuality, to the extent that it was adopted, into a broad range of other experiences and forms of behaviour, into the kind of person you were; it had as palpable an existence over against the individual as the conventions and life of the molly houses themselves, which it repeated on the personal scale.

It was thus both the root of the problem and in part its solution. It had been the extension of the meaning of homosexuality into areas previously unaffected by it that had made homosexuality qualitatively more apparent and vulnerable to persecution; and with that came a sharper choice and the guilt and alienation that attended it. But this extension of the meaning of homosexuality was also in part its own answer. At the same time it made it possible for the perplexed and harassed individual to find a refuge in an alternative society and identity where homosexuality had a coherent and central position. He could be a molly, the cause of his alienation and the means of overcoming it.

There is though something this does not explain. For all the violence with which this society repressed homosexuality, there is an ambiguity in its attitude, unacknowledged yet surprisingly easy to see. This is not the same as the ambivalence of Elizabethan and Jacobean society, its reluctance in most circumstances to recognise homosexuality for what it was. Without any parallels in the preceding period, the pogroms of the eighteenth century had a devastating effect, leaving behind them a trail of mass arrests and executions before a huge and jubilant mob.[40] A conviction for sodomy could — and often did — mean the death penalty, while a conviction for attempted sodomy was punishable by prison, a fine and the pillory, which could in itself be a sentence of death. In theory the crowd were not supposed to throw potentially lethal missiles: in practice this restriction was largely ignored, and the pillory could well mean serious injury or even death.[41] And yet the pogroms were only intermittent and were interspersed with long periods of relative calm during which the molly houses once again flourished. The unlucky or careless individual might still be arrested, but the molly houses themselves and the world they represented were not seriously challenged. The readily advanced explanation for this was that the molly houses were hidden; when they were discovered, they were cleaned up.

> Thus, without detection, they continued their odious society for some years, till their sodomitical practices were happily discovered by the cunning management of some of the underagents to the Reforming Society.[42]

So wrote Edward Ward in 1709 in his essay 'Of the Mollies Club', probably referring to the period before the suppressions of 1707. The same impression was repeatedly given by the constables and the agents for the Societies for the Reformation of Manners in the trials of 1726. It was the customary explanation; and yet it does not begin to stand up to investigation. After all, is it not highly improbable that the extensive network of molly houses across London — they and their associated culture — could have managed to remain hidden for so many years? How could such a thing have been hidden? And indeed there is evidence that they were not, at least as far as the population at large were concerned. At George Whitle's trial one of the witnesses explained how for several years he had known that Whitle's tavern was a molly house.[43] A second witness elaborated on this:

> For two or three years past it was commonly reported that the prisoner kept a molly house, and therefore the neighbours did not care to go and drink there.[44]

Similarly Margaret Clap's house was said to have 'the public character of a place of rendezvous for sodomites',[45] and to have been 'notorious for being a molly house'.[46] The scandalised neighbours of Margaret Clap and George Whitle knew quite well what these places were about. The authorities in the shape of the Justices may not have, and even the Societies for the Reformation of Manners may have had to search them out, but those who lived

From a broadsheet of 1762, showing a molly in the pillory. [41]

around them and the many who came across them were well aware of what they were. They were not 'hidden' in any real sense at all.

Why then were they left alone? Effectively, they were tolerated, although in a tense and hostile atmosphere; and that accords ill with the violence and downright savagery of the periodic pogroms. For all the protestations to the contrary, one cannot avoid the conclusion that they served a function wider than the needs of those who took refuge in them: that society, however ambivalent its attitudes, had an interest in them. The alternative identity and society they were taken up with had an ambiguous result, and here the explanation lies: they served, in effect, a dual purpose, for they must have restricted the spread of homosexuality at the same time as they secured its presence. To take on a new identity of this kind was a formidable prospect; for some altogether too much. If homosexuality had implications as broad as this, then for many it was not to be. Is the hostile but tangible toleration then so surprising? For the same reason that for some the molly houses provided a solution and a means of escape, for others they effectively closed the door: too much was involved. They thus served the needs of persecutor and persecuted alike.

But the stability they thereby achieved was only limited. Surely, there were only a few such places. They were not difficult to find; and they were vulnerable. Why then be content with containment? Why not pull them up by the roots and have done with them once and for all? That plausible chain of thought was the element of instability, and the result was an uneasy balance between two contradictory responses. It was at just this point that the Societies for the Reformation of Manners had their place; their role was to tip the balance, when they were able, from containment to the pogrom and genocide. Yet ultimately it was a hopeless task. There are times when, if your right hand does offend you, it is not possible to cut it off. This was one of these; for the molly houses were not a finite entity within society that could be cut out: they were a function of society itself. And so when the bloodletting was over, the pressures that had produced the molly houses in the first place began their work again; and once more they appeared and gained a precarious stability until another attempt was made to suppress them. Not only did the intermittent persecutions ultimately fail in their objective; ironically they added steam to the very pressures which were to recreate the molly houses after the overt persecutions had ceased, for it was just such manifest and unavoidable animus that made the molly houses so pressing a necessity. The long-term effect of the activities of the Societies for the Reformation of Manners was precisely the opposite of what they intended.

One looks in vain for any predecessor to the Societies for the Reformation of Manners; as with so much else that affected the social expression of homosexuality, they were a product of the closing years of the seventeenth century. Before that time there is a gap, a profound discontinuity. Across this gap the relationship between homosexuality and society emerges radically trans-formed. The changes which it brought and which I have endeavoured to outline in this chapter are complex, but in the word 'molly' we can see them brought together in a single crystal. It implies something different both from what preceded it and from what was to come later. In comparison to the terms which emerged in the nineteenth and twentieth centuries — such as 'homosexual', or the now obsolete 'uranian', or the contem-porary 'gay' — something is missing: it has none of the psychological expectations these words carry or the biological or even medical overtones that 'homosexual' for instance has had. It does not imply as they do a particular state of mind or physical condition; and in terms of its relation to ideas of masculinity and femininity, effeminacy does not occupy the same position in the homosexual identity today as it did in the 1720s.

But 'molly' also differs profoundly from its predecessors in Renaissance England, the words 'bugger' and 'sodomite'. In one sense it is more limited: unlike them, it is concerned with homosexuality alone, while they are about sexual confusion in whatever form, of which homosexuality was only one part. Yet it is also a broader word, in that 'molly', unlike 'bugger' or 'sodomite', involved more than sexuality in the most immediate sense alone. In it we can see encapsulated the expansion of the meaning of homosexuality described in this chapter to encompass behaviour that was not intrinsically sexual at all, to be the basis for a particular social identity, in short a molly. In that it was far more like the terms that were to come later; 'molly' and 'homosexual' for example are alike in that they refer to such a social identity, a kind of person, not the same identity but crucially *an* identity nevertheless. It marks a momentous change. What had been a thread throughout Elizabethan and Jacobean society became by the end of the century a subculture, a miniature society within a society, in its own right. And a largely nominal control had been replaced by an active persecution. What had once been thought of as a potential in all sinful human nature had become the particular vice of a certain kind of people, with their own distinctive way of life. The change is revolutionary, and there is one obvious and insistent question which can no longer be avoided: why?

It is a simple question but far and away the most difficult to answer; for the place homosexuality occupied in society as late as the England of the Earl of Rochester, however much we analyse it, appears entirely stable. Certainly homosexuality had a disruptive potential, as contemporaries were well aware, but that potential was resolved through a highly effective series of adjustments, often no more than nominal, which contemporaries were far less ready to acknowledge. Indeed it was a more adequate resolution than what prevailed by the close of the century. There is no apparent reason why it should have changed: yet it did. The only conclusion to be drawn is that the problem in understanding this is in the way the question is put: in terms of the history of homosexuality, there is no answer. The reason is, quite simply, that there is no linear history of homosexuality to be written at all, any more than there is of 'the family' or indeed of sexuality itself. These things take their meaning from the varying societies which give them form; if they change it is because these societies have changed. It is there that the explanation is to be found for the changes we have seen taking place during the course of the seventeenth century. We need to look away from immediate questions of sexuality and homosexuality and search out whether these changes had their parallels and companions elsewhere; and if we do that the final piece in the puzzle slides into place.

✣

Our fears are made in our own image. When, in a past society, the feared object is homosexuality, there is a mirror in which we can see reflected the society that rejects it; in the terms used, in the outline of what is being feared, lie the preoccupations and ways of thought of that society. And the greater the force of its rejection, the more naively it reveals itself. So when an Elizabethan theologian or Jacobean satirist used terms which placed homosexuality in relation to their intellectual universe, it is not surprising that they should describe it in ways characteristic of their time: it was universal, in the sense that in their minds it was a temptation common to our fallen human nature. It could not be a temptation for one but not another. 'Man' was 'not only the noblest creature in all the world, but even a very world in himself';[47] he was the microcosm and shared in all the weaknesses as well as the strengths of fallen humankind. Ultimately the explanation, or so an Elizabethan would have been inclined to put it, was in the nature of God, because even in its fallen state the universe would still always reveal in its identity of whole and part the oneness of its Creator. Certainly homosexuality was a temptation to be rejected with horror, as one would reject murder or apostasy and yet know that the root of the matter was in you. As such, potentially at least, its scope was universal. By the end of the seventeenth century these ideas have largely become history. What is now far more evident is that homosexuality is universal only among a particular kind of people, mollies: it was their vice. The change is one of viewpoint, from the typical and the general to the individual and the particular.

Changing ideas of homosexuality were by no means alone in this: '... abstract ideas,' wrote John Locke in 1690, 'removed ... from particular existence ... give us no knowledge of real existence at all ... all things that exist are only particulars.'[48] John Locke's *Essay Concerning Human Understanding*, from which these quotations are taken, is a sustained argument in philosophical terms for this change in understanding the nature of things. And in this it was only the most cogent expression of the new philosophical ideas of the time. Hobbes had already pointed out that there is 'nothing in the world universal but names, for the things named are every one of them individual and singular',[49] and Berkeley was later to conclude 'that every thing which exists is particular.'[50] These ideas matched without difficulty the new ideas on the nature of homosexuality which at the time became the norm: in this new atmosphere the ideas of an Elizabethan theologian on the subject would have seemed strangely out of place. In the England of John Locke as much as in that of Richard Hooker the way homosexuality was understood revealed the character and preoccupations of that society: and the outline was all the sharper for the failure to see that what they feared and rejected so fiercely was their own shadow.

But the relationship between philosophy and ideas of sexuality was hardly direct. Indeed the same habits of mind can be found scattered throughout the culture of the period in bewildering profusion. For example the same attitudes are clearly at work in its new — and characteristic — literary forms. In *The Rise of the Novel*,[51] Ian Watt has pointed out how the novels of Defoe, Richardson and Fielding were much more in tune with empirical philosophy than the allegories and romances which the novel replaced as popular fiction. Their original plots, individualised characters and realistic settings are in marked contrast to the romances, whose conventional characters inhabit a timeless world. It is the attitude to time that most clearly pinpoints the difference. It is significant that the word 'anachronism' first came into currency in English during the seventeenth century,[52] and that at the same time literary criticism acquired its modern form as the study of individual writers and schools, seen distinctly and in development, rather than of timeless poetic forms.[53] In the new late seventeenth century genre of the novel these attitudes are taken for granted; in them we breathe the air of the empirical philosophers. We can see the same process at work in the fortunes of another literary form which was in some ways similar to the romances: the emblem books, which during the course of the century ceased to be regarded as a serious branch of literature.[54] The emblem books were collections of allegorical pictures, often highly complex, accompanied by expositions in verse. The intellectual pleasure they gave — the wit — in unravelling their complex meanings was a serious, even a learned, pleasure; and they were enormously popular in the late sixteenth and early seventeenth centuries. Yet by the end of the century this was a literary form thought of, if at all, as merely light entertainment or as a source of children's books. They chart very neatly the change in mentality. To be taken seriously one had to take seriously their universal significance. They were timeless, not only in their temporal incoherence — in that they would happily crowd together into one picture events which clearly occurred not together but in sequence — but also in that they operated within a view of the world as ordered and unchanging, from which the same universal truths could — indeed must — be drawn over and again: the snake swallowing its own tail to form a perfect circle, the traditional image which George Wither twice used in his *Collection of Emblemes* as an illustration of the cyclical nature of time, setting out ceaselessly the same unchanging truths.[55] The emblem books declined when the credibility of allegory waned, for they had always been only one expression of an intense interest in allegory to be seen throughout Renaissance England — in interior decoration, in clothing, in ceremonial as well as in literature. But what gave allegory its weight and significance was that, more than mere artifice and deeper than the surface of life, it was taken as uncovering the foundations upon which the world had been built.

'Nature,' explained Richard Hooker, 'is nothing else but God's instrument . . . We see then how nature itself teacheth laws and statutes to live by.'[56] By the end of the seventeenth century the attitude this presupposes is strikingly absent from English society: it was John Locke and empirical philosophy which now expressed the radically altered — and to us far more familiar — approach of their time. Truth was to be found by the investigation of the observer, the individual reflecting on the evidence of his senses: we should each ideally be a Newton who, 'in his never enough to be admired book, has demonstrated several propositions, which are so many new truths, before unknown to the world.'[57]

Truth understood, as here, in the way empirical philosophy wanted it understood, in terms of development and singularity, required a pluralism that would have been quite alien to Richard Hooker and his contemporaries. The ideas of indefinite progress and development, for example, which are now so much a part of the modern world, began to appear only in the later seventeenth century;[58] they involved an openness to novelty and variety entirely in keeping with the period. There is a remarkable illustration of this in the delayed reaction to the discovery of the New World which J.H. Elliott has described.[59] It is striking how little influence in the sixteenth and seventeenth centuries the discovery of America had on Europe's intellectual horizons. Classical cosmographies which the new discoveries had shown to be misleading and out of date continued to be regularly reprinted and used in the schools. The works of art brought to Europe from the New World were treated as wonders to be admired but not as models which could influence Europe's own art. And as Professor Elliott remarks, 'it is difficult not to be impressed by the strange lacunae and the resounding silences in many places where references to the New World could reasonably be expected'.[60] It was only after 1650 that European philosophy began to consider seriously the intellectual implications of the discovery of America. It required a pluralism which the age provided.

And if there was a multiplicity of worlds on Earth, why not in the heavens? At the same time as the implications of the discovery of the New World were being grasped in Europe, the long-standing philosophical debate as to whether or not there was a plurality of worlds or universes was finally resolved, and in similar terms.[61] The argument had had partisans on both sides ever since the days of Democritus and Aristotle, but the dominant conclusion of Medieval and Renaissance philosophy was that there was only one world. The arguments were varied, and at times ingenious, but at their root they were a consequence of the belief in the oneness of God: the unity of God,[62] Thomas Aquinas argued, proved the unity of the world, His creation. The discovery of the telescope came as a serious blow to this view: it showed that the moon and, by analogy, the other planets, were Earth-like spheres, and shifted the argument, in a way that was to prove fatal to the unitary answer, away from the possibility of a series of universes to the apparent existence of a plurality of Earth-like worlds. That the change should have occurred during the course of the seventeenth century is not at all surprising: given the openness to ideas of variety and multiplicity in the late seventeenth century, the question was unlikely to survive as a philosophical problem. In his *Dioptrica Nova* published in 1709 William Molyneux went a step further and asked, seeing we now know the moon is an Earth-like body, that we 'think awhile, whether all these celestial bodies that thus dance round our Sun may not be inhabited?' Saturn, for example, may be cold and Mercury hot, but — he goes on to suggest — may there not be 'varieties of creatures...some adapted to one planet, others to others?'[63] A plurality of worlds and a variety of creatures: a conclusion to be understood in the context of the Scientific Revolution of the late seventeenth century, but no less symptomatic of its time for all that.

The late seventeenth century shows a striking change in mentality, in popular ways of thought, of which the new conceptions of homosexuality described in this book were a part. At the same time as homosexuality began to be conceived of as a characteristic of certain individuals only and not of others, we can find a wealth of evidence of the same frame of mind at work in areas as diverse as philosophy and popular literary forms, astronomy and geography. It should not surprise us. Renaissance conceptions of homosexuality were deeply enmeshed in the intellectual and mental world of their time; when the one changed, so did the other. And the new ideas of homosexuality that appeared in England towards the end of the seventeenth century are not isolated phenomena: they are part of the emergence of that concern with the individual and the particular which is peculiarly modern.

But while the archetypical figure in which the Elizabethans and Jacobeans embodied their ideas of homosexuality had little direct relation to the facts of social life, this was by no means true of the molly: that figure was part of everyday experience. We need to explain something more than why homosexuality was now conceived of in this form. We also need to explain its social extension in the culture of the molly houses. Clearly of course the form this took — a plurality of worlds within the social body — suggest that there was some connection and something to be explained. The explanation is partly in the fate at the time of monolithic social forms, which survived no more easily into the late seventeenth century than did universalist habits of mind. The most spectacular example is the state itself, the absolutist state of the Renaissance prince, parasitic, bureaucratic and overgrown. As Hugh Trevor-Roper has so brilliantly shown,[64] the economic and administrative challenges of the seventeenth century were to prove fatal to it. Some went quietly by attrition and reform, others in disaster and revolt in the social upheavals that swept across Europe in the middle years of the century: Catalonia and Portugal in 1640, Naples in 1647, France in 1648, the Netherlands in 1650, and the most far-reaching of all in 1642, when the English Civil War broke out and arguably the most gorgeous and unyielding of all Renaissance princes came to catastrophe. And with the Renaissance state perished the equally absolutist Renaissance church. When Strafford fell, so did Laud; but it is crucially important to grasp that all the warring religious parties of Stuart England — Anglican, Puritan and Catholic alike — shared the same ideal of one universal Church; the number of sectaries, who did not share this ideal, was miniscule before 1642. But the religious proliferation of the Interregnum, the appearance of sects which had no desire to be part of a state church, provided the groundwork for change: the unbending

Anglicanism of the Clarendon Code and the toleration of nonconformists after 1688 did the rest. By the end of the century an independent and variegated nonconformist culture coexisted peacefully alongside the established church and the ideal of a single national and universal Church had become the theological abstraction it was to remain.

By the end of the seventeenth century the twin pillars of the Renaissance state and the Renaissance church, equally inclusive in their claims to authority, had crumbled. But the process was more complex than this might suggest: both were involved in a culture that was undergoing a crisis broader than issues of government and ecclesiastical organisation. To take the church as an example, its changes of fortune involved more than the *de facto* abandonment of the ideal of a national church: rather this period sees the ousting of religion itself from major areas of thought where previously it had claimed a right to be heard. The expulsion was done with reverence: this was no age of atheism. But it was none the less real for that. John Locke, for example, argued for the continuing importance of faith and religious belief but defended them by means which relegated them, for their own defence, to a much narrower scope. In the section of his *Essay* entitled 'Of Faith and Reason, and their distinct Provinces', the rival claims of each are satisfied by the total distinction of the provinces in which they are deemed appropriate:

> First, whatever proposition is revealed of whose truth our mind by its natural faculties and notions cannot judge that is purely matter of faith and above reason.
> Secondly, all propositions whereof the mind, by the use of its natural faculties, can come to determine and judge from naturally acquired ideas are matter of reason.[65]

Effectively, religious language was being abandoned as an appropriate medium in important and basic areas of investigation; and that was at a time when the goal of a single national church wedded to the state was being rejected as a practical or even desirable ideal. In this twin process, involving on the one hand the church and on the other religion, we can see the underlying unity of the intellectual and social changes of this period. They were fundamentally part of the crisis of a culture.

The landscape that emerges is far more familiar to us than what preceded it. As the turmoils of the mid-century die away, the

England we see is startling changed. Religion is no longer the natural language of science and politics. Ideas of microcosm and macrocosm, of the Great Chain of Being, and other expressions of divine order in nature that appear or are hinted at so often in Renaissance writings as to seem a habit of mind, disappear from all but poetic fancy or strictly theological discourse. What replaces them is a far more familiar milieu: Newton's *Principia*, the Royal Society, a rational management of the economy, and mechanical conceptions of nature recognisably modern. Images and mental habits which had persisted for centuries virtually disappear: demonology and witchcraft trials, for instance, reached a climax in the late sixteenth and early seventeenth centuries but then faltered and had ceased in practice long before the repeal of the Witchcraft Act in 1736.[66] The size of the change can of course be exaggerated: early eighteenth-century English society was not the same as our own. The scientific advances of the late seventeenth and early eighteenth centuries were largely theoretical and speculative; the mechanical techniques that were to make possible the Industrial Revolution and the social changes that was to bring lay in the future. Yet when we look at the society of England under Elizabeth I or James I its strangeness only deepens as we probe its working; and if we look at that profoundly altered England of the late seventeenth century and think at times we catch glimpses of the origins of the world in which we live, we are right, for they are indeed there.

It is difficult to give a single all-embracing explanation for these changes. Perhaps it is naive to seek one. With historical change on as broad a scale as this, it is not always clear whether what one is looking at is cause or effect; was the Scientific Revolution for example the cause of the materialistic ideas that accompanied it, or were they the precondition for it? To identify one element as formative in this broad process and the rest as mere superstructure is a presumptuous exercise. Certainly what is clear though is that the nature of these changes is illuminated to only a very limited extent by the social upheavals of the mid-century. These were movements at least as much of protest or reaction as of self-confident assertion; and few if any of the new attitudes that were to emerge can be attached to one or other of the contending parties. The changes that lay beyond the upheavals were related rather to the disintegration of the social fabric which made the emergence of a new kind of culture possible, perhaps even imperative.

'The seventeenth century,' wrote Herbert Butterfield in *The Origins of Modern Science,* 'indeed, did not merely bring a new factor into history, in the way we often assume — one that must just be added, so to speak, to the other permanent factors... We know now that what was emerging towards the end of the seventeenth century was a civilisation exhilaratingly new perhaps, but strange as Nineveh and Babylon.'[67]

In that atomised and pluralistic society, strange to the world it replaced but not to us, conceptions of homosexuality in a recognisably modern form first appear; they are part of it, as the traditional conceptions of homosexuality they replaced had been part of an earlier society. At the same time as the idea of a plurality of worlds was becoming a readily acceptable notion, whether literally on the other planets or figuratively in the New World or within English society, so homosexuality was also coming to be thought of as the distinguishing characteristic of a separate, sexually nonconformist, culture; and to a considerable extent was actually being expressed as such. As the generally accepted image of the sodomite was transformed from a figure which was not a person but an archetype to one particular kind of individual, so we can see the same mentality at work in the imaginative literature of the time, in the replacement of timeless and stylised literary forms by the realistic and particularised figures of the novel. The older forms were simply no longer credible. In Locke's philosophy we can see that judgement explicitly justified. That is why empirical philosophy leaves the uncanny impression that it can be read, without ever mentioning the topic, as explanation and justification for the new conceptions of homosexuality. Of course this was not what Locke was writing about; but he was expressing in generalised terms the newly developed culture of which these ideas and his philosophy were a part. The sodomite as the attendant of witches and demons, as the force of anarchic disorder set against divine Creation he was once conceived of, is now an alien idea: but the England of Newton and Locke is far more familiar, as the world of the molly houses is familiar to anyone who knows the homosexual subculture in London today; and for the same reason.

Professor Stone has shown at length how the individualism of late seventeenth-century English society affected also heterosexual relationships, in the growth of what he has termed 'affective individualism', the transition from 'the more kin-, client-, and community-oriented and more financially bonded family of the late middle ages' to 'the more private, more domestic and affectively bonded family of the eighteenth century'.[68] The related changes in homosexual relations were a parallel development, a related but separate response to the broader cultural changes which Professor Stone recognises as the context for the change in heterosexual relations he describes. There were indeed other forms of deviancy than the sexual, and late seventeenth-century society reacted to them in equally characteristic ways. The early decades of the eighteenth century saw the rapid spread of a new social institution: the workhouse.[69] Its ostensible purpose was to take over from the parishes the distribution of poor relief, but it contained more than the poor; along with them were the mentally ill and — for the workhouse was also a place of deterrence and correction — the 'sturdy beggar'. It is an institution entirely characteristic of the new social order: this had devised a means which, as in its response to homosexuality, removed the aberration, in this case the recalcitrant and the mentally ill, from the mainstream of society. The new conceptions of homosexuality and the new social forms in which they were expressed were not a reaction to other changes in sexuality: they appeared as part of a broader crisis in the relationship of society and the individual.

On a warm summer's evening in 1726 a man was arrested on the open ground near the City called the Moorfields. That night two constables had gone out, in the immediate aftermath of the trials and executions of that year, to see if further arrests could be made. The infamous Thomas Newton was with them; and their intention was to use him to entice and trap another man on the Moorfields, which they knew to be a homosexual meeting-place. Thomas Newton played his part; and they made their arrest, a man by the name of William Brown. That night was to end for him in imprisonment, the pillory, and probably, as a married man, the ruin of his life. In court he watched his words carefully, but when he was faced with arrest and the violent abuse of the constables he spoke with more feeling. It is hardly surprising. He had known Thomas Wright, who had recently been executed for sodomy, and he had lived — and survived — with so many others the tensions and fears of the previous twelve months.

'I did it because I thought I knew him,' he replied, 'and I think there is no crime in making what use I please of my own body.'[70]

It is difficult to imagine an arrest in similar circumstances a century earlier; but even if this were possible, could one imagine the victim saying that? It is not that William Brown's claim was any more acceptable in 1726 than it would have been in the England of Edward Coke or Richard Hooker; but was not his defiant assertion that his body was his own now more credible, more symptomatic of his time? Such a claim can be made in any age, but to have made it in Jacobean England would have meant shaking off the accepted conventions and beliefs of society to a far greater extent than it required a century later; so great that one wonders whether, if it had been made, it would have been understood and recorded. William Brown's response tells us at least as much about those who recorded it as the man who made it.

The appearance in England of a separate homosexual culture and a distinctive homosexual identity were part of that far-reaching transformation which English society underwent in the course of the seventeenth century, a transformation which played its part in making the world in which we now live. The figure of the homosexual, either as we see it there in its first and early form among the molly houses or as it is now after more than two centuries of change, has never been a welcome part of the society, the atomised pluralistic society, which gave rise to it. But it is its reflection.

Afterword

This book now appears in a context very different from the one in which it was first published, thirteen years ago. At the time of its publication, from an academic point of view this book was an oddity, its subject little considered by historians; indeed its writing was no academic project but rather a personal obsession, done largely in isolation and mostly late at night after a day's work as a British career civil servant. The lack of scholarly interest in this subject has been transformed: homosexuality in sixteenth- and seventeenth-century Europe is now widely discussed in a growing stream of books, scholarly articles, and doctoral theses.

The purpose of this afterword is not to explain why such a change came about but rather to explain, with the benefit of hindsight, why this book had the success it did. This work had its effect because it fitted its moment, by making a number of mutually reinforcing connections whose time to be recognized had come. One was intellectual, in the association it made between the practice of writing history and the influences the study drew on in contemporary sociology and linguistics. To this was added the potential it represented for a union between a politically aware academia and the vibrancy of the new movements for homosexual emancipation of the 1970s and 1980s. With these we may include its appeal to both a scholarly and a popular readership.

The book might not have been so successful, were it not for the warm welcome given it by several major historians and literary critics, including Hugh Trevor-Roper, Christopher Hill, and Anne Barton. It also benefited greatly from later detailed discus-

sion of its ideas in the writings of Jonathan Goldberg, Eve Sedgwick, and others. Much gratitude is due for that crucial initial
support. Thanks also to that great institution the London Library, which was founded (with the enthusiasm of Thomas Car-
lyle) in 1840 on the still shocking assumption that if scholarship
is not to be the reserve of professionals, then the stacks have to
be open and the books taken home.

The critical test for this book came in the years immediately
following its publication. These saw the publication of research
carried out in several European archives on the extensive documents they contain, previously largely disregarded by historians, that deal with prosecutions for homosexuality from the
fourteenth to the eighteenth centuries. Such studies supported
the thesis put forward in the final chapter of this book, especially the parallel developments described by Michel Rey for
eighteenth-century Paris and by Theo van der Meer for
eighteenth-century Holland. The work of James Steakley suggests that a similar conclusion is probably true of contemporary
Prussia also, while a paper by L. J. Boon illuminatingly shows
the older notions of homosexuality coming into direct confrontation, to catastrophic effect, with the newer notions I describe
in a village in the Netherlands in 1731. In southern Europe the
transition was less marked, for, as we can now see from the
work of Rafael Carrasco, Guido Ruggiero, and Luiz Mott, homosexuality was both more evident in social forms of its own
and less apt to be passed over by the quiet nominal adjustments
of Renaissance England. Southern Europe nevertheless shared
many of the same assumptions about homosexuality as northern Europe. Michael Rocke's book on homosexuality in
fourteenth- to sixteenth-century Florence had not appeared at
the time of this edition and will clearly be a work of the first
importance, as will be the forthcoming publication of Theo van
der Meer's definitive study of homosexuality in the Netherlands, *Sodom's Seed in the Netherlands: The Emergence of Homosexuality in the Early Modern Period.*

In this book I have attributed the changes described to the
growth of individualism in late-seventeenth-century England
and to the emergence in the England of that time of a pluralistic
modern society. This idea has been echoed and greatly developed in the writings of Randolph Trumbach on eighteenth-
century Europe, in which to my mind he very persuasively

places the emergence of a homosexual identity within wider changes in European culture and in the relations between the sexes.

Other scholars have pointed out the evidence for a more gradual transition than was apparent to me thirteen years ago. The first was Christopher Hill, the veteran British socialist historian, who in a review of this book (later expanded and included in his collected essays) drew attention to the similarities between ideas of sexual individualism and the radical political claims that were heard in England in the 1640s and 1650s. He suggests that the molly houses may have had an origin some decades before their existence was made plain by the murderous persecution instigated by the Societies for the Reformation of Manners. Bruce Smith and Gregory Bredbeck both have published important studies drawing out the preconditions emerging from the end of the sixteenth century for the appearance of a homosexual identity. Each sees this as a potential rather than as necessarily actualized. Smith in particular is at pains to describe the extent to which this potential was in tension with its context, and Bredbeck is importantly less concerned with its actualization than its deployment in creating *heterosexuality* as a distinct form of eroticism, a point allied to Randolph Trumbach's argument for recognition of the extent to which the appearance of the modern homosexual role has served to support heterosexual social institutions.

The questions discussed in this book have begun to give way now to other and different questions. I feel no embarrassment in saying this, for one of the tests of a book is not how many questions it answers but how many it prompts. Subsequent research of this kind has been most successful in following the illumination attitudes to male homosexuality may cast on wider relations between men in the society of sixteenth- and seventeenth-century England, whose conventions of masculine friendship and political bonding have proved particularly susceptible to such an approach. The seminal work in this respect was the analysis of the cultural significance of Shakespeare's sonnets in Eve Sedgwick's *Between Men: English Literature and Male Homosocial Desire*. It is an approach that has been developed to spectacular effect in Jonathan Goldberg's essays, most of which have been collected in his *Sodometries*. In these he draws out both the reluctantly acknowledged affinity in this society between the bonds of male friendship and male homosexuality and the lethal use made in the early modern period of the language of homosexuality in the emerging ideologies of colonialism and imperialism. The encompassing context of such social links between men also figures prominently in Bruce Smith's book. Neither Guido Ruggiero nor Rafael Carrasco explicitly makes this link, although much of the material they draw on would have been easily described by a contemporary as "friendship." In these contexts the quiet adjustments of northern Europe would have been near to hand, an argument that I have put forward in a review of Guido Ruggiero's book and that coincides with Rafael Carrasco's comments on the way homosexual relationships could be discreetly integrated into the life of the household.

The difficulty this culture had in distinguishing between the desired and the feared bonds between men is also the direction my own subsequent work has taken. A first fruit of this approach was a paper originally published in *History Workshop Journal* in 1990 on homosexuality and the signs of male friendship in sixteenth-century England.

In retrospect, it is much easier now to place this book in its context than it was when it made its unheralded appearance in 1982. It is not the previously hidden history of a supposedly "homosexual" minority (although it is a previously unwritten chapter in the history of the English working class, from which I come). Indeed one of its primary motives was to disabuse the reader of that notion of a homosexual minority. Nor is it a history designed to emancipate sexuality. Its drive was rather to play a part in toppling King Sex from the throne he has occupied too long. It is not even a history of sexual practices. With the modesty and caution I know is proper, my hope is that its relevance is potentially more universal. The writing of this book and the body of research that has been joined to it have persuaded me that attitudes to homosexuality unquestionably have been symptomatic of fundamental changes in European society and in substantial part constitutive of them.

Notes

Quotations from primary sources, whether from modern or original editions, are given according to the following rules. Spelling, punctuation (except where the text is written in formal periods), and the use of capitals have been modernised. Abbreviations have been expanded, except where they serve a metrical purpose. Proper names have been standardised and modernised. I have not preserved italic type. Words inserted to make up the sense and words deleted in the original are placed in square brackets; the latter are specifically noted. Obsolete forms, which I have modernised, are noted where they could be open to debate or where they are interesting in themselves. A note is given wherever I have felt it necessary to emend the text.

Titles of books, etc., have not been modernised; nor have verb forms.

All dates are given with the year beginning on 1 January.

Crown copyright material in the Public Records Office is reproduced by permission of the Controller of H.M.S.O.

Notes to Introduction

1 Ellis *Studies in the Psychology of Sex; Part Four: Sexual Inversion.* There is a similar presentation of the Renaissance in Carpenter *The Intermediate Sex* pp. 45-7.
2 Garde *Jonathan to Gide;* Rowse *Homosexuals in History* There is a related neo-Freudian interpretation in Taylor *Sex in History.*
3 Karlen *Sexuality and Homosexuality;* Bingham *Journal of Interdisciplinary History* Vol.1 pp. 447-68; Bullough *Sexual Variance in Society and History.*
   On the medieval background, see Boswell *Christianity, Social Tolerance and Homosexuality;* Goodich *Unmentionable Vice;* Bailey *Homosexuality and the Western Christian Tradition;* Bullough *Sex, Society and History* pp. 74 ff.

On homosexuality elsewhere in Europe, see Ruggiero *Journal of Social History* Vol.8 Summer pp. 18-37; Monter *Annales Économiés Sociétés Civilisations* Vol.29 pp. 1023-33.

On North America, see Katz *Gay American History;* Oaks *Journal of Social History* Vol.12 pp. 268-81; Crompton *Journal of Homosexuality* Vol.1 pp. 277 94.

On other aspects of sexuality in Renaissance England, see Laslett *The World We Have Lost* and *Family Life and Illicit Love in Earlier Generations;* Laslett and Wall *Household and Family in Past Time;* Stone *Family, Sex and Marriage in England 1500-1800;* Quaife *Journal of Social History* Vol.11 pp.228-44 and *Wanton Wenches and Wayward Wives: Peasants and Illicit Sex in Early Seventeenth Century England.*

4   On Mary McIntosh and Jeffrey Weeks, see note 1 to Chapter 3 and note 18 to Chapter 4.

Notes to Chapter One

1   *1 Corinthians* chapter 6, verse 9, *Authorised Version 1611* and *Revised Standard Version 1952.* The two Greek words are μαλακοί and ἀρσενοκοῖται . See also Chapter 3, note 77 below, and Boswell *Christianity, Social Tolerance and Homosexuality* pp. 106-7 and 335-53.

2   Weeks *Coming Out* p.3.

3   Coke *Third Part of the Institutes* p.58; see also *Twelfth Part of the Reports* p.36.

4   *Sodom Fair* p.28.

5   Winthrop *History* Vol.2 p.55.

6   *Deuteronomy* chapter 23, verse 17 (margin), *Authorised Version.*

7   Butler *Hudibras* p.110; Dryden *Dramatic Works* Vol.1 p.106; Jordan *Cheaters Cheated* quoted in Dryden *Dramatic Works* Vol.1 p.430; Wilmot *Poems* pp.48 and 130; Wheatley *London* Vol.1 p.506.

8   Du Bartas *Divine Weeks* (trans. Sylvester) pp.518 and 522.

9   *Life and Death of John Atherton.*

10   Wilmot op. cit. p.41.

11   Donne *Satires* p.18.

12   Marston *Poems* p.112.

13   Jonson *Jonson* Vol.8 p.34.

14   Coke *Third Part of the Institutes* p.59. Coke is adapting *Ezekiel* chapter 16, verse 49.

15   Drummond *Poetical Works* Vol.2 p.298.

16   Turbervile *Tragical Tales* p.372.

17   Middleton *Epigrams and Satyres* p.9.

18   Rainolds *Th' Overthrow of Stage-Playes* pp.10 and 32.
18a Bradford *Plimouth Plantation* p.459.
19   See note 7 above.
20   ditto.
21   Lindsay *Works* Vol.3 p.243.
22   *Of the Horrible and Woful Destruction of, Sodome and Gomorra.* It
     depicts the sexual sins of Sodom and Gomorrah only in the most
     general terms, as debauchery rather than homosexuality, which is
     not specifically mentioned.
23   On this general topic see p.80 below.
24   In Dunbar *Poems* pp.85 and 94.
25   Coke *Twelfth Part of the Reports* p.36; 'sodomites': I have
     modernised Coke's 'sodomers'.
26   Lithgow *Rare Adventures* pp.12 and 229.
27   See note 4 above.
28   Lindsay *Works* Vol.1 p.345.
29   Goodich *Unmentionable Vice*; Bullough *Sex, Society & History*
     pp.74 ff; Boswell op. cit. pp.283-6, and Chapter 3 note 79 be-
     low.
30   Lithgow op. cit. pp.306-7.
31   Fish *Supplication* pp.63-4.
32   Marston op. cit. pp.112-13.
33   Pagitt *Heresiography* p.139. John White used the traditional
     identification of homosexuality with heresy from a Puritan
     position to vilify the Laudians in his *First Century* A2v and
     A3.
34   Coke *Third Part of the Institutes* p.58. See also *Twelfth Part of the
     Reports* p.37. Coke is paraphrasing a passage in *The Mirror of Justices*
     p.15.
35   Danchin *Revue Germanique* 1913 (Nov.-Dec.) pp.566-87; *English
     Literary Autographs* (ed. Greg) no.XV. On Baines see Boas *Times
     Literary Supplement* Vol.48 p.608.
36   Danchin pp.571 and 571-2. The second is crossed out in the
     copy, presumably to shorten it. False coining is also associated
     with homosexuality in James I Βασιλικὸν Δῶρον.
     p.38 and Du Bartas op. cit. p.525.
37   Danchin pp.570 and 572, and p.570. The second remark is crossed
     out in the copy; see note 36 above. 'Sodoma': Latin for Sodom.
38   Danchin pp.570 and 572. The Popish associations are reinforced by
     reference to Richard Cholmley, a Papist sympathiser (see Danchin
     pp.571, 572 and 575-8).
39   Karlen *Sexuality and Homosexuality* p.117 notes the traditional
     association in the allegations of sexual deviance with heresy and
     treason and on this basis questions their reliability. Although
     Baines clearly chose his material with care and probably influenced

its wording, there is reason to think that these alleged remarks do reflect Marlowe's opinions: there is independent evidence of Marlowe's 'atheism' (Greene *Groats-worth of Witte* pp.43-4, Eccles *Notes & Queries* Vol.169 pp.20-3, 39-41, 58-61 and 134-5 and Danchin op. cit. pp.567-70); two of the minor individuals named can be identified, Cholmley and Poole (see note 38 above and Eccles *Times Literary Supplement* Vol.33 p.604); Marlowe is linked in the allegations to Sir Walter Raleigh whose circle seems to have held similar views (Danchin pp.570, 574, 576, and 578-87, Nashe *Works* Vol.1 p.172, Aubrey *Brief Lives* Vol.1 pp.284-7 and Vol.2 pp.188-9, Parsons *Responsio* in Boas *Marlowe* p.113, Raleigh *Works* Vol.2 p.548-56).

40   Macfarlane *Witchcraft in Tudor and Stuart England* p.6; Trevor-Roper *Religion, The Reformation and Social Change* p.95; Russell *Witchcraft in the Middle Ages* p.29; Bullough op. cit. p.75, and generally Thomas *Religion and the Decline of Magic.* My concern here is with the fantasies of demonology rather than with the mythology of witchcraft accusations; accusations of witchcraft in England show far less evidence of the belief in the witch's sexual intercourse with the Devil than in other parts of Europe, where the sixteenth-century witch craze had greater influence.

41   Oldham in Wilmot *Collected Works* pp.95-6; on authorship see Vieth *Attribution in Restoration Poetry* pp.72 ff.

42   R.C. *The Times' Whistle* p.79.

43   Drayton *Works* p.169.

44   Drayton op. cit. p.174.

45   Drayton op. cit. p.174.

46   *The Life and Death of John Atherton* A4v.

47   Du Bartas op. cit. p.523.

48   Drayton op. cit. p.170.

49   Trevor-Roper op. cit. p.184.

50   Browne *Religio Medici & Other Works* p.15.

51   Browne op. cit. p.174.

52   Browne op. cit. p.29.

53   Milton *Poetical Works* p.313.

54   Shakespeare *Complete Works* pp.672 and 829.

55   Browne *Works* p.19.

56   Quoted in Tillyard *Elizabethan World Picture* p.25, translated from the Latin.

57   *Genesis* chapter 1, verse 1.

58   Drayton *Works* Vol.1 p.167.

59   Turbervile op. cit. p.388 and 389. Turbervile's description (p.372) is:

Perhaps the moujik hath
  a gay and gallant wife:

To serve his beastly lust, yet he
  will lead a bugger's life.
The monster more desires
  a boy within his bed
Than any wench...
A moujik is a Russian peasant. I have modernised the obsolete
forms 'Mousick' (moujik) and 'bowgard' (bugger) used by
Turbervile.

60 Hooker *Works* Vol.1, p.200.
61 Hooker op. cit. Vol.1, p.208.
62 Bradford op.cit. pp.459-60.
63 Lindsay op. cit. Vol.1 p.235.
64 Taylor *Works* p.444.
65 Dante *Divine Comedy* Vol.1 pp.72ff and Vol.2 pp.224-5.
66 Scottish Record Office/JC/1/13. Included in the partial
    transcription in Pitcairn *Criminal Trials* Vol.3 p.491.
67 Greater London Record Office/MJ/SR/521/179.
68 Coke *Third Part of the Institutes* p.59 and *Twelfth Part of the
    Reports* p.37.
69 Thomas op. cit. p.638.
70 Bossy *Past and Present* 1962 pp.39-59.
71 Thomas op. cit. pp.647 and 667-8.
72 Coke *Third Part of the Institutes* pp.58-9.
73 e.g. Baines in Danchin op. cit. pp.570 and 572: 'he used him as the
    sinners of Sodoma.'
74 I have used the typescript edition *Sodom or the Quintessence of
    Debauchery* prepared by Patrick J. Kearney and deposited in the
    British Library. On authorship see Baine *Review of English Studies*
    Vol.22 pp.201 ff. The play has also been attributed to John
    Wilmot, Earl of Rochester; while it is difficult to see why the
    authorship of the obscure Christopher Fishbourne should have
    been substituted for Rochester's, it is not surprising that the
    reverse should have occurred. The play's obscenities have
    distracted attention from its literary qualities: an ironic
    juxtaposition of tragedy, satire, surrealistic pornography and a
    traditional story treated in an untraditional way. It deserves more
    critical attention than it has received. However the importance of
    the play for the history of homosexuality has been exaggerated; the
    ostensibly homosexual theme no doubt shocked conventional
    opinion, which was what it was intended to do, but the play's
    eroticism is entirely heterosexual. This is something one has always
    to be on the watch for when evaluating contemporary references to
    homosexuality in the Restoration. Thomas Shadwell (*Works*
    p.253) relates a story of John Dryden, when he was 'in the company
    of several persons of quality' at Windsor; asked how they might

pass the afternoon, he scandalised the party by suggesting: 'Let's
bugger one another now, by God!' Shadwell acidly comments:

> He boasts of vice (which he did never commit);
> Calls himself whoremaster and sodomite;
> Commends Reeve's arse and says she buggers well;
> And silly lies of vicious pranks does tell.

A similar caution needs to be used in evaluating the homosexual
elements in the poems of the Earl of Rochester.

75 See Freeman *English Emblem Books.*
76 Lindsay op. cit. Vol.2 pp.197-386.
77 Lithgow op. cit. p.364.
78 Bingham, *Journal of Interdisciplinary History* Vol.1 pp.455 and
    459. He was adapting *Leviticus* chapter 18, verse 25.
79 *Arraignment and Conviction of... Earl of Castlehaven.*
80 Browne op. cit. pp.33, 15 and 69.
81 See pp.16-17 above.
82 Trumbach *Journal of Social History* Vol.11 Fall pp.1-33.

Notes to Chapter Two

1   *Registers of the Company of Stationers* ed. Arber pp.677-8.
2   Marston *Poems* pp.77-8.
3   Drayton *Works* pp.173-4.
4   Jonson *Jonson* vol. 8 pp.34-5; Brathwaite *Times Curtaine Drawne*
    p.F7v; Guilpin *Skialetheia* A5-A5v, A8, B1v; E2; Donne *Satires* pp.
    4, 18, 44, 52; Middleton *Works* Vol.8 p.21. See also Marston *Poems*
    pp.112, 140-1, 145. On English Renaissance satire generally see
    Peter *Complaint and Satire in Early English Literature* and Kernan
    The Cankered Muse.
5   Peter op. cit. pp.99-103.
6   Stubbes *Anatomie of Abuses* p.166.
7   R.C. *The Times' Whistle* p.79.
8   Trumbach *Journal of Social History* Vol.11 Fall p.9; Weeks *Coming
    Out* p.35; Boswell *Christianity, Social Tolerance and Homo-
    sexuality* pp. 31-7.
9   Braudel *Capitalism and Material Life* p.431; Gregory King's
    estimate of the population of London in 1688 was 530,000.(Laslett
    World We Have Lost p.55.)
10 Braudel op.cit. p.378.
11 Laslett op. cit. pp.137-8.
12 Where the Middlesex Sessions do differ however is in the relatively
    large number of sodomy cases that appear in them in comparison to
    similar records elsewhere; is this evidence for the view that
    homosexual contacts were more widely available in London? The
    number of cases is certainly striking. Le Hardy's *Calendar* covering

the Middlesex Sessions of the Peace 1 December 1612 to 20 March 1618 includes four sodomy cases (see pp. 72-3 below), while for example a search in the Essex Quarter Sessions archives 1556-1680 did not produce a single case of this kind (Macfarlane University of London M.Phil. thesis 1968 pp.139 and 180). On the rareness of sodomy cases in court records generally see pp. 70-1 below. However it is questionable whether general patterns of sexual behaviour can ever be deduced from court records, with any credibility (see p.41 below). Nor do such patterns need to be brought in as an explanation here. When we look at the circumstances of the four cases in Le Hardy's *Calendar*, they do not appear to be markedly different to sodomy cases from outside London, which is not what one would expect if they were the product of different patterns of sexual behaviour. Taking each in turn, one involved violence (Alban Cooke; Le Hardy *Calendar* Vol.1 p.110); another appears to have been a malicious prosecution (Edward Bawde; op. cit. Vol.3 p.33); a third was the result of a parental complaint (Peter de Guy; op. cit. Vol.4 p.312): the background to the fourth (Gabriel Pennell; op. cit. Vol.1 p.115) is obscure. These are typical features of sodomy cases generally: where it is possible to identify why particular sodomy cases came to court, there is usually sign of their having involved some breakdown in social relations (see pp. 71-2 below). It was this which was accentuated by the strains of London's rapid growth rather than homosexuality *per se*.

13 See Zagorin *The Court and the Country*.
14 This is the context in which we should take the complaints of homosexuality concerning James I and his court. What is implied by Osborne in his *King James* pp.127-8 (and by Weldon in his *The Court and Character of King James*, pp.59 and 125) is bluntly stated by Peyton in his *Divine Catastrophe*, (in *Secret History of the Court of James I* Vol.2 pp.301-466, see pp.346 and 348). The complaints were written with a similar political intention, summed up by Osborne:

> He, like Adam, by bringing the Crown into so great a necessity through a profuse prodigality became the original of his son's fall (op. cit. p.2).

On the homosexual element in James's life, see the beautiful and sensitive biography by Caroline Bingham *James I of England*.
15 Laslett op. cit. p.87 and *British Journal of Sociology* Vol.27 pp.319-42.
16 Cockburn *Journal of the Society of Archivists* Vol.5 (1974-1977) pp.215-231 and 'Trial by the Book?' in *Legal Records and the Historian* ed. Baker pp.60 ff.
17 Cockburn in *Legal Records and the Historian* op. cit. p.62.

18   Greater London Record Office/MJ/CP/1/221. Calendared in Le
     Hardy *Calendar* Vol.1 p.110.
19   Greater London Record Office/MJ/SR/521/179. Calendared in
     composite form together with source cited in note 18 above in Le
     Hardy op. cit.
20   Public Record Office/Assizes/24/21 (69v)-(70). The marginal note
     reads: 'Domingo Cassedon Drago to be sent unto Essex gaol to be
     tried for a buggery, and the evidence to be sent thither.' In the text
     'Domingo' is 'domyngo', an alteration from a crossed-out word
     which appears to be 'Domyngo'. 'Negro': I have modernised the
     form 'negar' throughout. 'For' is deleted after 'there'. Calendared
     in Cockburn *Western Circuit Assize Orders* p.247.
21   Cockburn op. cit.
22   See Ruggiero *Journal of Social History* Vol.8 Summer p.19. For a
     contrary view, which I find unconvincing, see Quaife *Wanton
     Wenches* p.5.
23   Laslett op. cit. pp.53-80.
24   Public Record Office/Assizes/35/49/4 mm 22, 44, 45, 67. Calend-
     ared in Cockburn *Calendar of Assize Records Hertfordshire
     Indictments James I* pp.34 and 37. The details in the indictment are
     supported by those in the recognizances.
25   Public Record Office/Assizes/35/22/9 m40. Calendared in
     Cockburn *Calendar of Assize Records Sussex Indictments Elizabeth
     I* p.156.
26   White *First Century* p.1.
27   Sussex Record Office/QR/EW 57 (60)-(65). On John Wilson see
     also *Journals of the House of Commons* Vol.3 p.271; Walker
     Sufferings of the Clergy pp.406-7; Tatham *Dr. John Walker and the
     Sufferings of the Clergy* p.203; Matthews *Walker Revised* p.362;
     Sussex Archaeological Collections Vol.11 pp.1-49, Vol.36 p.156;
     Sussex Record Society Vol.12 p.39, Vol.14 pp.242-3, Vol.54 pp.xxii,
     16, 205, 209; and p.64 below. I have accepted John White as being,
     on balance, a reliable guide to John Wilson's unorthodox sexuality.
     However, White does need to be used with caution. His reliability
     on this point is challenged in *Persecutio Undecima* pp.26-7, a
     royalist tract published in London in 1648:

     ... and let any man judge if that first and only example of
     buggery prove not *John White* and his abettors the true
     sons of the Father of Lies, who was a liar from the
     beginning; for either the party was found not guilty, why
     then sequestered? Or guilty, why then not punished by
     death according to law?
           It is not to be imagined that the Puritans would conceal
     the shame of any clergyman, when they so raked each
     dunghill and corner to discover it, but that such an instance

(if proved) should have been triumphantly stretched to further their glorious Reformation; and whether the party so accused was not some   years before this Parliament cleared by the Justices of the Peace for Sussex, who sifted out that Puritans' plot against him (as one of those Justices told me), I refer the reader to the then Justices of that county.

Also, it is surprising to discover from the Quarter Sessions depositions (op. cit.) that the Samuel Andrews mentioned by John White as an object of John Wilson's sexual interest and presumably one of his sources is none other than the Puritan tailor who was instrumental in having John Wilson prosecuted at the Quarter Sessions for his political views. However there is reason to think that in this respect White's book is an accurate source: this is the only example of homosexuality White's book contains and it lacks the stereotyped formulas he uses elsewhere; when John Walker was gathering material for his history of the ejected ministers, John Wilson's scandalous life was still remembered in the area over fifty years later (Bodleian/Ms. J. Walker/c. 20/460v; the relevant passage is transcribed in Tatham op. cit. p.203); the Quarter Sessions depositions also bear out in detail John White's report of John Wilson's political views.

28 Laslett op. cit. and Laslett and Wall *Household and Family in Past Time.*
29 Stone *The Family, Sex and Marriage in England 1500-1800.*
30 Laslett and Wall op. cit. p.152. These figures are derived from a survey of 100 pre-industrial communities. Only 15 of these were examined at a date before 1700, but the figures published separately for Ealing (Middlesex) in 1599 suggest there is no reason to think that analyses taken at dates before 1700 would show a smaller preponderance of servants than those taken later. In Ealing at this date out of a total population of 427 individuals 25.5 per cent of the population were servants (Laslett and Wall op. cit. p.82).
31 ditto p.147.
32 Laslett *Family Life and Illicit Love in Earlier Generations* pp.34 and 44.
33 On this subject generally see Laslett *World We Have Lost;* Flandrin *Families in Former Times;* and Smith *Past and Present* Vol.61 pp.149 ff.
34 Hajnal in *Population in History* ed. Glass and Eversley pp.101 ff; and Laslett *World We Have Lost* p.82.
35 Laslett *Family Life and Illicit Love in Earlier Generations* pp.214-32.
36 Quaife *Journal of Social History* Vol.11 p.231. See also note 41 below.

37 Morgan *New England Quarterly* Vol.15 pp.597-600.
38 See pp.70-1 below.
39 Somerset Record Office/Q/SR/62. Partially transcribed in Quaife *Wanton Wenches and Wayward Wives* p.175. See Chapter 3, note 34.
40 Scottish Record Office/JC/1/13. Included in the partial transcription in Pitcairn *Criminal Trials* Vol.3 p.491 note 2.
41 Quaife op. cit. in note 36 above which gives his results in detail. Quaife's study is based on a sample of 500 bastardy cases from the Somerset Quarter Sessions records 1645-1660; 'on most issues the specific evidence is available for from one- to two-thirds of the sample' (p.242). The result is therefore, as he says, impressionistic. See also Quaife op. cit. pp.229-30 and *WantonWenches* pp.59-88.
42 Aubrey *Brief Lives* Vol.1 p.71; D'Ewes *Autobiography and Correspondance* Vol.1 p.192.
43 Spedding *The Letters and the Life of Francis Bacon* Vol.1 p.244.
44 Bingham *Journal of Interdisciplinary History* Vol.1 pp.447- 68.
45 Middleton *Works* Vol.8 p.21. An 'ingle' was an expression denoting the same as 'catamite'; it usually implied a social inferior. (Though it did not always do so: Guilpin's Pollio — a character who appears in his poems — is said to have an 'ingle's face' but is also described as a wealthy young man whose debts are set to drive him out of town; Guilpin *Skialetheia* p.A8.)
46 Brathwaite *Times Curtaine Drawne* p.F7v.
47 Wilmot *Poems* p.51.It is not clear to what extent the speaker represents the poet and to what extent he is a persona adopted by him as in note 48 below.
48 Wilmot ditto p.117.
49 Wilmot *Valentinian* in *Collected Works* pp.161-238. Fletcher *Works of Francis Beaumont and John Fletcher* p.21.
50 See pp. 70-4 below.
51 Greater London Record Office/MJ/SR/472/131, SBR/1/133,CP/ 1/69. I have used the manuscript calendar in the Greater London Record Office.
52 Laslett and Wall *Household and Family in Past Time* p.82.
53 Stone *The Family Sex and Marriage in England 1500-1800* pp.517; expanded in Pelican ed. p.322-3.
54 R.C. *The Times' Whistle* p.80.
55 Marston *Poems* pp.112-13. On Marston's influence on *The Times' Whistle* see Kernan *The Cankered Muse* p.128, as well as the obvious verbal parallels.
56 On Udall, see *Proceedings and Ordinances of the Privy Council* Vol.8 pp.152-3. On Cooke, see Emmison *Elizabethan Life* p.47 (quoting from the court books of the Archdeaconry of Colchester).
57 Donne *Satires* p.4.

58 Florio *Queen Anna's New World of Words* p.88.
59 Marston *Poems* p.112; this is in the form of an ironic defence. There
    is also a reference to male brothels ('malekind stews'), although not
    in a directly contemporary context, in Drayton *Works* Vol.3 p.174.
60 Walker *Relations and Observations* Book 2, Second Part p.257: the
    'new-erected sodoms and spintries at the Mulberry Garden at S.
    James's'. On 'spintry' in the sense of a homosexual brothel, see *The
    Oxford English Dictionary* 'Spintry'. The Mulberry Garden was on
    the site apparently now occupied by Buckingham Palace:
    Chancellor *The Pleasure Haunts of London* pp.201-5.
61 Quaife *Wanton Wenches* pp.146-52.
62 Marston *Poems* p.78.
63 See note 6 above.
64 Guilpin *Skialetheia* p.B1v.
65 Drayton *Works* p.173.
66 Hutchinson *Memoirs* p.84.
67 *The Oxford English Dictionary* 'Mimic'.
68 Jonson *Jonson* Vol.IV p.209.

Notes to Chapter Three

1 On the sociological issues that underly this chapter, see Plummer
   Sexual Stigma and *Making of the Modern Homosexual* ed. Plummer
   pp.17-29; McIntosh 'The Homosexual Role' in *Social Problems*
   Vol.16 pp.182-92, reprinted with postscript in *Making of the
   Modern Homosexual* op. cit. pp.30-49; and Lemert *Human
   Deviance*. (I have been particularly impressed by Lemert's
   distinction between 'primary' and 'secondary' deviation, pp.17-18
   and 40-64.) These approaches have been perceptively developed,
   largely in connection with the history of homosexuality in the
   nineteenth century, in Weeks *Coming Out*, *History Workshop*
   (Vol.1 pp.211-19); *Radical History Review* (Vol.20 pp.164-79);
   Making of the Modern Homosexual (op. cit. pp.76-111);
   Homosexuality: Power and Politics (ed. Gay Left Collective, pp.11-
   20) and *Sex, Politics and Society*.
2 Du Bartas *Divine Weeks* p.500.
3 ibid. p.525.
4 See pp.7-8 above. For a more accurate description of Renaissance
   antagonism to homosexuality see Karlen *Sexuality and Homosexuality* pp. 120-1; Ruggiero *Journal of Social History* Vol.8 pp.18-
   37; Bingham *Journal of Interdisciplinary History* No.1 pp.447-68;
   Macfarlane *Regulation of Marital and Sexual Relations in
   Seventeenth Century England* pp.1 and 136-40.
5 Browne *Religio Medici* pp.70 and 74.
6 Drummond *Poetical Works* pp.43, 109 and 135.
7 ibid. p.298.

8   Ellis *Studies in the Psychology of Sex* Vol.1 pp.42-3; Garde *Jonathan to Gide* pp.329-30.
9   Barnfield *Poems* ed. Arber.
10 ibid. p.44.
11 Barnfield *Complete Poems* ed. Grosart pp.xxxiii-xxxiv and 198-220.
12 Coke *Third Part of the Institutes* p.58.
13 Lindsay *Works* Vol.1, p.345.
14 *English Literary Autographs* ed. Greg Part I no.xv.
15 *Life and Death of John Atherton* p.A4v.
16 Bradford *Plimouth Plantation* p.459.
17 Du Bartas op. cit. p.518.
18 James VI Βασιλικὸν Δῶρον pp.37-8, quoted in Bingham op. cit. pp. 460-1.
19 See p. 20 above and notes 35-39 to Chapter One.
20 Aubrey *Brief Lives* pp. 188-9.
21 op. cit. (note 14).
22 Danchin *Revue Germanique* 1913 p.570; the slight differences in the copy prepared for the Queen (p.572) are not significant.
23 Marlowe *Complete Works* pp.519-33 and 536-7.
24 Rowse *Homosexuals in History* p.31.
25 On paiderastes see Huloet *Abcedarium* Diiiv and Tiiv; and Coke *Third Part of the Institutes* p.58 and *Twelfth Part of the Reports* p.37. It is the use of the classical expressions in Aubrey's life of Francis Bacon (Aubrey op. cit. p.71) that gives the passage its neutral tone: 'He was a παιδεραστής. His Ganymedes and favourites took bribes; but his lordship always gave judgement *secundum aequum et bonum.* His decrees in Chancery stand firm, i.e. there are fewer of his decrees reversed than of any other Chancellor.'
26 Drayton *Works* Vol.3 p.174.
27 Marston *Poems* p.117:
        Nay shall a trencher slave extenuate
        Some Lucretia rape and straight magnificate
        Lewd Jovian lust, whilst my satiric vein
        Shall muzzled be not daring out to strain
        His tearing paw? No gloomy Juvenal,
        Though to thy fortunes I disastrous fall.
    'Jovian lust' taken on its own need not relate exclusively to homosexuality, if at all; but heterosexual rape and homosexuality were easily associated concepts (see p.14-16 above), and the reference to the fate of Juvenal indicates that Marston had homosexuality in mind. Juvenal was supposed to have suffered because of his strictures against homosexuality (see note by Davenport in ibid. p.301).

28 Winthrop *History* Vol.2 p.324.

29 White *First Century* pp.1-2. On Wilson see note 27 to Chapter Two.

30 I am thinking of mental adjustments such as: depreciating the experience as 'not important'; redefining it in terms of 'physical release' or friendship; or being unwilling to talk about the experience or to allow it to influence behaviour.

31 See pp. 74-8 below.

32 See pp.19-23 above.

33 See pp.42-9 above.

34 See p.48 above. Somerset Record Office/Q/SR/62. Quaife *Wanton Wenches* p.175 transcribes part of the boy's evidence but does not incorporate any material from that of Davy or that of the servant, Richard Bryant, who slept in the same room.

35 See pp. 42-57 above

36 White op. cit. p.1.

37 John Wilson's marriage license, from the Act Books of the Court of the Dean of Chichester, is calendared in *Sussex Record Society* Vol. 12 p.39.

38 Weldon *Court and Character of King James* pp.125-6, quoted in Rowse op. cit. p.63; *Dictionary of National Biography* Vol.2 pp.170-1.

39 Winthrop op. cit.

40 Somerset Record Office/Q/SR/40, partly transcribed and summarised in Quaife *Wanton Wenches* pp.175-7, although Quaife does not include the reference to Dowdeney being married.

41 Coke *Third Part of the Institutes* p.58.

42 Macfarlane op. cit. (but see also ibid p.22).

43 Quaife *Wanton Wenches* pp.175-7; he asks (p.246): 'Were they rare events or a regular pattern normally ignored by the judicial juggernaut?' My answer, as argued in this chapter, is definitely the latter. There was a greater incidence of cases in the Middlesex Sessions of the Peace, as discussed in note 12 to Chapter Two. However the number of cases in Le Hardy's *Calendar* (four in more than five years, and one of these — Gabriel Pennell — may refer to bestiality rather than homosexuality) is still in absolute terms very low, especially as the Middlesex Justices met eight times a year rather than the customary four because of the few criminal cases heard in the Middlesex Assizes and King's Bench. The number of homosexual cases is insignificant compared to the interest the Middlesex Justices took in heterosexual immorality.

44 Cockburn *Calendar of Assize Records*. At the time of going to press, the volume for Essex in the reign of James I had not appeared; but judging by Macfarlane op. cit. this will not contain any indictments involving homosexuality. The volume for Surrey

in the reign of Elizabeth I contains only one such case, and that for
Surrey under James I has not yet appeared. See also *Crime in
England* ed. Cockburn p.58.

45   Trevor-Roper *Religion, the Reformation and Social Change* pp.165-
     6 makes the same point in connection with the witch-craze.

46   See pp. 40-1 above.

47   There is an extensive example of this in Sir Thomas Herbert's
     narrative of his journey through Africa and Asia in the early
     seventeenth century, which repeatedly links homosexuality with
     non-European races, *A Relation of Some Yeares Travel.*

48   Scottish Record Office/JC/1/13, noted in Pitcairn *Criminal Trials.*
     Vol.3 p.491

49   *Life and Death of John Atherton;* Bernard *Penitent Death;* Wood
     Athenae Oxonienses Vol.2 pp. 891-3; Ware *Bishops of Ireland*
     revised Harris pp.539-41; *Dictionary of National Biography*
     Vol.2 pp.217-8.

50   Greater London Record Office/MJ/SR/543/202, quoted in Le
     Hardy *Calendar* Vol.3 p.33.

51   Greater London Record Office/MJ/SR/546/138 and SBR/2/266,
     calendared in Le Hardy op. cit. Vol.3 p.122.

52   Greater London Record Office/MJ/SR/554/109 and SBR/2/351
     and 359, calendared in Le Hardy op. cit. Vol.4 p.5.

53   Greater London Record Office/MJ/SBR/1/579, calendared in Le
     Hardy op. cit. Vol.1 p.9.

54   Greater London Record Office/MJ/SR/543/28-29 and SBR/2/236,
     calendared in Le Hardy op. cit. Vol.3 p.25.

55   Similar motives may have prompted the servant mentioned earlier
     (pp.68-9) who slept in the same room as Meredith Davy and who
     was instrumental in starting off the prosecution against him. Also
     the consciousness of a possible motive of this kind was probably
     present in one of the questions put to a witness in George
     Dowdeney's case (see p. 70) and preserved in his deposition:
     'and [he] saith that there was not ever any falling out or difference
     between the said Dowdeney and this examinate.' (Somerset Record
     Office/Q/SR/40.) This is not included in Quaife op. cit., note 40
     above.

56   Greater London Record Office/MJ/SR/521/179 and CP/1/221,
     calendared in Le Hardy op. cit. Vol.1 p.110.

57   See pp.68-9 above

58   See note 124 to Chapter Two.

59   Greater London Record Office/MJ/SR/562/63, 153, 169, 189, and
     CP/2/137v, calendared in Le Hardy op. cit. Vol.4 p.312.

60   Somerset Record Office/Q/SR/40 (partly transcribed and
     summarised as noted at 40 above, although none of the passages
     quoted below are included). My conclusion that it was Dowdeney's

advances to the boy that were the immediate cause of the prosecution is only an inference. Against it, the boy's father when recounting an experience he had had with Dowdeney some fourteen years earlier said only that 'he spake not thereof unto anyone ever since until about a week last past, and thinks he should never have spoken thereof but that now of late he heard divers others charge him with facts of the like kind.' Also according to the boy the incident was 'about St James's day last past', i.e. almost certainly the feast of St James the Apostle on 25 July 1621, while the boy's evidence is dated 17 April 1622. However the boy's father would obviously have wanted to play down the suggestion that what had happened with his son was colouring his own evidence, and the introduction to the boy's deposition implies that this incident was indeed the principal element in the prosecution: 'The examination of John Lyle the younger son of John Lyle before examined... concerning the crime of buggery whereof the said Dowdeney standeth accused'. There is no parallel to this in the other depositions.

There are a number of other incidents which were probably the result of similar circumstances. It is reasonable to assume that parental complaints were also at work in the prosecutions of Roland Dyer (Cockburn *Calendar Kent Indictments Elizabeth I* p.88) and Remily Clerke (Cockburn *Calendar Sussex Indictments Elizabeth I* p.261), who were each accused of homosexual offences involving boys. In the prosecution of William Bence (Cockburn *Kent Indictments Elizabeth I* p.341) the individual with whom he was supposed to have had homosexual relations is named but was not prosecuted, and one can reasonably conclude that he was either only a child or that William Bence had used violence. A fourth instance is that of George Willes who was complained of in the archdeaconry of Surrey in 1623 for what was probably a homosexual offence involving a boy, 'for the abuse of which child and scandalising of the parents' he was excommunicated (Greater London Record Office/WJ/SR/12/128 and 129. I have used the manuscript calendar in the Greater London Record Office).

61 A related conclusion was reached by Quaife *Wanton Wenches* pp.178-83 as a result of his study of illicit sexuality (largely heterosexual) in seventeenth-century Somerset.

62 See p.52 above. Stone (*Family, Sex and Marriage* p.493) notes the 'singular lack of anxiety' shown by parents to the end of the seventeenth century about the homosexual influences their sons might be subject to at school or university.

63 England was certainly different as far as witch persecution was concerned. Apart from a short period in the 1640s, the witch craze with its elaborate demonology and mass persecutions did not take root in England.

64 Monter *Annales Économies Sociétés Civilisations* Vol.29 pp.1023-33.
65 Lithgow *Rare Adventures* p.335.
66 Another illustration of this is the striking absence of any interest in homosexuality among the sexual radicals of the Interregnum period. Pagitt *Heresiography* carefully chronicles the alleged sexual libertinism of the sectaries but mentions homosexuality only in connection with the Jesuits. See also Hill *World Turned Upside Down*.
67 Lithgow op. cit.
68 Herbert op. cit.
69 Turbevile *Tragical Tales* p.372.
70 Browne *Religio Medici and other Works* p.60: Browne inserted the phrase into an imperfect quotation from Sonnet lxviii of Joachim du Bellay's *Les Regrets* (Ward *Review of English Studies* Vol.5 pp.59-60).
71 Coke *Third Part of the Institutes* p.58. See also *Twelfth Part of the Reports* p.37.
72 Coke *Third Part of the Institutes* p.58. See also *Twelfth Part of the Reports* p.36: 'Nota, bugarone Italice is a buggerer, and buggerare is to bugger, so buggery cometh of the Italian word.'
73 See note 60 above.
74 The master was a 'mariner' and was probably at sea.
75 See note 34 above.
76 ibid. 'Since': I have modernised the 'sithence' given in the original.
77 Trumbach (*Journal of Social History* Vol.11 Fall p.11) rejects this view: 'It is possible to collect enough other evidence to show convincingly that whenever homosexual behaviour surfaced at the royal courts, from the 12th to the early 17th centuries, it was accompanied by what contemporaries viewed as markedly effeminate behaviour.' Certainly there is evidence for this: Marston (*Poems* p.145) refers to 'yon effeminate sanguine Ganymede'; Osborne (*King Iames* pp.127-8) describes James I's favourites as being highly effeminate; and in his translation of Du Bartas (*Divine Weeks* p.340) Sylvester implied that the Sodomites and their allies were transvestites. (Susan Snyder (ibid. p.845) interprets the obscure reference involved:

No (Zeboiim) here are no looking-glasses
For para-nymphs to gaze their painted faces

as 'Sylvester meant men pretending to be nymphs, i.e. acting like women.' However the close parallels between these lines and 'Ingling Pyander' in Middleton's *Micro-Cynicon* (*Works* Vol.8 pp.130-4) indicates that Sylvester had specifically in mind the transvestism of Renaissance London which Middleton vividly describes.) But one can just as easily point to material where effeminacy is associated with heterosexual not homosexual immorality. A clear example is Nicholas Breton's verbal sketch in his *The Good and the Badde* of 'An Effeminate Foole' (*Works*, pp.12-13 of *The Good and the Badde*), whose sexual vices as Breton describes them are entirely heterosexual. That is Breton's point: the 'effeminate' young man he is caricaturing has become so obsessed with his mistress and indolent feminine ways that the robust manly virtues have been forgotten. Indeed one of the distinctive meanings of someone being 'effeminate' in the seventeenth century, a meaning which was obsolete by the end of the century, was that he was much given to women, usually with disapproving sexual overtones (*Oxford English Dictionary* Vol.3 'Effeminacy' 2., 'Effeminate' *a.* and *sb.* 3., and 'Effeminateness' 2.) This is the meaning John Donne (*Satires* p.52) is ironically referring to in his epigram:

Thou call'st me effeminate, for I love women's joys:
I call not thee manly, though thou follow boys.

In all these instances, whether they involve homosexuality or heterosexuality, effeminacy is associated with luxurious living and sexual vice in general, which is primarily what is implied, not homosexuality alone. Marston, Guilpin, Brathwaite, Middleton and Drayton all make much of the clothes, behaviour and lifestyles of the sodomites they describe, but there is nothing specific to homosexuality in their descriptions: they were not intended to convey homosexuality alone but sexual and material indulgence in general. When the biblical translators of 1611 see p.13 above translated μαλακοί (literally softness, primarily of touch but by extension of people and their mode of living also) as 'effeminate' and linked with it the specifically homosexual translation of the accompanying word ἀρσενοκοῖται ('abusers of themselves with mankind'), they neatly expressed the associations any sexual vice had for them, homosexual and heterosexual alike.

78 Hajnal in *Population in History* ed. Glass and Eversley pp.101 ff; Laslett *World We Have Lost* p.82 and *Family Life and Illicit Love* p.26.

79 Boswell *Christianity, Social Tolerance and Homosexuality* pp.267-332, which sets out in detail the evidence for a sharply increased intolerance of homosexuality in late twelfth-century Europe. All of the forms in which this intolerance appeared, as Boswell describes it, can be paralleled in sixteenth- and seventeenth-century England: the association of homosexuality with non-European races, heresy and treason; the unreserved maledictions of theologians; its prohibition in secular codes of law; and its use in political accusations. Boswell also notes, however, how little evidence there is of the courts enforcing legislation against homosexuality (pp.281

note 39, 289, 290 note 58, 293-5 including note 74) but makes far
less of this material than of the literary and circumstantial evidence
of increased hostility to homosexuality. Nor does he draw any
broader conclusions from the legal material. He is unlikely to have
told the whole story. The social mechanisms I have described need
not have applied in the late Middle Ages or outside of England, but
their presence in this later period in a similar form to the material
Boswell has described raises serious doubts about the extent to
which the sharply increased intolerance he has identified actually
impinged on daily life.

80   Trumbach op. cit. pp.2-9 and notes 67, 68 and 69 above.
81   See pp.17-19 above, and Chapter Two passim.

Notes to Chapter Four

1   The description of the molly houses given in this chapter has been
reconstructed from the accounts of the trials in *Select Trials*
(referred to below as *S. T.*), Vol.1 pp.105-8, 158-60, 280-2, 329-30;
Vol.2 pp.257-9, 362-72; Vol.3 pp.36-40, 74-5. I have supplemented
these by the literary descriptions in the Preface to the *Tryal and
Condemnation of ... Earl of Castle-Haven; Women-Hater's
Lamentation* (this source was kindly brought to my attention by
Professor Randolph Trumbach); Dunton *He-Strumpets;* Ward
History of London Clubs pp.284-300; *Hell upon Earth, Satan's
Harvest Home* pp.45-61. This chapter is not put forward as a
complete description of the molly houses: my intentions have been
restricted to illustrating, by contrast, the changes that occurred in
the social expression of homosexuality during the course of the
seventeenth century. There is an excellent and full description of
the molly houses in Trumbach *Journal of Social History* Vol.11 Fall
pp.11-33.

The Preface to the first volume of *Select Trials* claims that the
accounts have been compiled from three sources:

The most considerable part of the trials are immediately
transcribed from original notes taken in court ...

The rest are selected from the sessions papers; and here
we have closely followed the sense of the printed copies;
though, to render the matter in evidence manageable and
clear, the depositions, which are there given in the third
person, we have chosen to deliver in the first.

We have examined and compared a large collection of
papers, both printed and manuscript, relating to the lives of
several whose trials are here published ... (p.A2v).

These volumes should not be taken uncritically. They were
intended as a form of entertainment; and their editors naturally

gave prominence to the sensational aspects of the molly houses, as indeed did the prosecution at the trials themselves. There are also reasons for thinking that some of the prosecution's evidence was concocted. Its reliability is several times challenged (*S.T.* Vol.1, p.281; Vol.2, pp.365 and 370); individuals such as Thomas Newton or Ned Courtney (p.90 below) would hardly have been above this. Although not conclusive, it should also be borne in mind that in some of these trials the defendants were acquitted; and at least one of the prosecutions seems to have been brought wholly for malicious reasons (that of Thomas Rodin in Vol.1, pp.280 ff). However, while one may doubt the reliability of particular details, the picture that emerges of the molly houses as a whole is almost certainly reliable. It is impossible to believe that a compilation of this size could have been a fabrication; it is far too consistent, both within itself and with the literary accounts, as well as with the contemporary newspapers used by Trumbach in his article (op. cit.), for it to be other than substantially accurate. The position is probably best summed up in what Thomas Wright said to the chaplain before his execution: 'He said also that Newton swore falsely against him; but could not deny his following these abominable courses...' (*S.T.* Vol.2, p.369).

   With the literary material similar problems of a bias towards the sensational have to be borne in mind. On Ward op.cit. see note 15 below; on Dunton op. cit. see note 24 below.

2   Rocque *Plan of the Cities of London and Westminster;* Lehman *Holborn* pp.61 and 112.
3   *S.T.* Vol.3, p.37.
4   Fryer *Mrs Grundy* pp.103-5.
5   'Molly' in the homosexual sense of the molly houses etc. was taken over from Molly, a form of the female name Mary: it was part of the effeminate conventions of the homosexual subculture.
6   *S.T.* Vol.2, p.368; Thomas Wright's house in Beech Lane.
7   *Hell upon Earth* p.42; this does not explicitly say that the brandy shop in Charing Cross was a molly house, but it is a reasonable inference. The other molly houses are referred to in the narratives of the trials in *S.T.*
8   *Hell upon Earth* p.43; on St James's Park see note 9 below; for an arrest in the Moorfields see *S.T.* Vol.3, pp.39-40; there is a possible reference to another such spot in Dunton op. cit., p.95.
8a *S.T.* Vol.3, p.36
9   Wilmot *Poems* p.41, quoted on p.14 above. The poem was already in existence by 20 March 1673, when it is referred to in a letter documented by Lucyle Hook *Modern Language Notes* Vol.75, p.480.
10 For example William Brown, who 'had been married 12 or 13 years'

and who was indicted for attempted sodomy in 1726. (*S.T.* Vol. 3, pp.39-40.)

11   *S.T.* Vol.2, p.371.
12   *S.T.* Vol.2, p.365.
13   *S.T.* Vol.3, p.74.
14   *S.T.* Vol.2, p.371, George Whitle.
15   Ward op. cit. p.284. This contains a long description of a mock birth and baptism, including a baptismal dinner complete with mock wifely speeches (followed by an orgy); pp.285-8. This has often been taken at its face value (including Trumbach op. cit. p.17). However a ritual as elaborate as this is unsupported by other evidence; it is surely a fanciful and sensational invention based on the effeminate slang and transvestism of the molly houses.
16   *S.T.* Vol.2, pp.257-8.
17   Middleton *Works* Vol.3, pp.130-34. On the meaning of effeminacy in sixteenth- and seventeenth-century English society see Chapter Three, note 77.
18   The emergence in England by the early eighteenth century of a homosexual subculture and a homosexual identity was first pointed out by Mary McIntosh; see references in Chapter Three, note 1. This has been challenged, with reservations, by Jeffrey Weeks: *History Workshop* Vol.1, pp.211-19; *Coming Out; Radical History Review* Vol.20, pp.164-79; *Homosexuality: Power & Politics* ed. Gay Left Collective pp.11-20; *The Making of the Modern Homosexual* ed. Plummer pp.76-111; *Sex, Politics and Society*. In these works he argues that the crucial period in the emergence of the modern homosexual identity and subculture was nearly two hundred years later, in the late nineteenth century. The word 'homosexual', as he points out, is a product of this period; he relates this to the parallel development of the medical model of the homosexual in nineteenth-century psychology, to the concern in legal circles from the 1860s to distinguish homosexual offences within the catch-all crime of 'buggery', and to the passing of the Labouchère amendment in 1885 (which for the first time in English law supplemented the concept of 'buggery' by explicitly criminalising homosexual acts as such). The context for this in his view is the elaboration in late nineteenth-century England of a multiplicity of new sexual categories: the homosexual alongside the professional prostitute, the housewife, and the adolescent, disseminated in the case of the homosexual by the labelling effect of the new medical and legal categories and of several popular scandals at the time involving homosexuality, notably that of Oscar Wilde. The elevation of the family in the writings of the social purity campaigners served to heighten the distinction between acceptable and non-acceptable forms of behaviour and added to this effect.

In Weeks's earlier work, which is in a Marxist tradition, these changes are explained as being consequent upon a restructuring of the family to meet the needs of victorious nineteenth-century capitalism. It needs to be emphasised though that his later work goes beyond orthodox Marxism and is both more subtle and less schematic. He still recognises economic and consequent social changes as the preconditions and ultimate limits of the development he is describing, and sees the nineteenth century as crucial. But he is now more willing to envisage a variety of influences and an uneven process over time; and he explicitly rejects a purely economistic approach or one based on a simple class analysis. He is also now concerned to stress the differing ways homosexuality could be socialised and the paradoxical elements in these new sexual categories, in that although restrictive they could become at the same time focal points of self-affirmation and resistance to that restriction, the homosexual reformers at the end of the nineteenth century being a clear case in point. Weeks acknowledges here the influence on him of the writings of Michel Foucault. He shares with him a view in which sexuality is not, as in the traditional Marxist model, a biological drive restricted by capitalism, but a more neutral element in the life of the body, structured and classified in specific situations: i.e. *given* an importance rather than repressed and diverted. The historical development of homosexuality Foucault puts forward in his *History of Sexuality* is similar to Weeks's; Foucault envisages an elaboration of sexualities, of 'discourses' on sexuality, beginning in the sixteenth century and coming to its final stage at the end of the nineteenth when medical and juridical concepts of 'perversions' can clearly be seen taking over from earlier moral categories of debauchery.

There is an interesting comment on this view in John Marshall's article in *The Making of the Modern Homosexual* ed. Plummer pp.133-154. Firstly, he points out the extent to which discussion of homosexuality in traditional terms of moral decline and unregulat -ed male lust continued well into the post-Second World War period, and secondly he argues that the homosexual identity has traditionally been a matter of ideas of gender rather than (as is now largely the case) of alternative types of sexual orientation; in each case the change takes place, in his view, well into the twentieth century. He attributes these developments to the partial relaxation of gender roles in the post-War period and to more liberal attitudes to sexual pleasure. Unfortunately his article, although suggestive, is an impressionistic mosaic of comments culled from personal interviews, Parliamentary debates, medical writings and journ-alism, and alone it is not conclusive.

All of these four writers are at one though in seeing homosexuality not as a transhistorical, biologically determined entity, but as a plastic element in human life susceptible to historical and social moulding to an extreme degree. While disagreeing with all four on certain admittedly important points of detail, this book is written in the same tradition and owes much to the stimulus of these writings.

My principal point of departure is from the crucial role Jeffrey Weeks assigns to the nineteenth century. The means as Jeffrey Weeks describes them by which the new homosexual role was disseminated should give rise to doubt. Is it credible that medical and legal practice, however greatly changed, together with the writings of social purity campaigners and a series of scandals, could have had so profound an effect, and that ultimately on social groups which could have known little or nothing of them? Moreover, is it credible that their effect should have persisted long after the causes themselves had largely been forgotten? If so, then the effect is out of proportion to the cause. These doubts are strengthened by what Jeffrey Weeks has to say about the molly houses of the eighteenth century. He recognises that the existence of a homosexual subculture a century or more before the nineteenth century does not fit well with a theory which sees the nineteenth century as the crucial turning-point. His reply is to undercut the seriousness of the problem in a way I find unconvincing: the molly houses were, he argues, merely an 'embryonic' subculture (*History Workshop* op. cit., p.213), 'emergent rather than ... developed' (*Coming Out* p.37), and lacking a distinctively modern form. The 'only frequent or regular participants' in the molly houses 'were the relatively few "professionals"' involved in prostitution (*Sex, Politics and Society* p.110). Prostitution was certainly a feature of the molly houses, but its class composition — predominantly lower and lower-middle class (see pp. 85-6 above) — suggests that prostitution did not have a central role; a regular participant was more likely to have been like William Griffin, an upholsterer in his forties who had been unsuccessful in business and was a lodger in a molly house for nearly two years. Jeffrey Weeks's explanation seems to me to be an inadequate description of the complex and intricate culture described in this chapter or in Randolph Trumbach's article (op. cit.). Indeed, the factors by which Weeks explicitly distinguishes the homosexual subculture of the nineteenth century from that of the molly houses — 'recognised cruising places and homosexual haunts, ritualised sexual contact and a distinctive argot and "style" (*Radical History Review* op. cit. p.166; *Making of the Modern Homosexual* op.cit. p.84) are amply present in the earlier period, although taking at places different forms.

Jeffrey Weeks's achievement is to have illuminated, firstly, the new psychological and medical understanding of the homosexual identity that gained ground at the end of the nineteenth century and its relation to the proliferation of new sexual categories, a process which is still going on; and secondly he has shown the connection between this and the contemporary changes in the law relating to homosexuality: each, as he shows, represented forms of regulation and control. But these were changes played out against an identity and minority homosexual culture that already existed and had done so, as I argue in this chapter, for two hundred years. By telescoping the two elements in the process he has obscured its ultimate origins, which must be looked for long before Victorian England – in the very different conditions of the closing decades of the seventeenth century.

19   *Hell upon Earth* p.43.
20   *S.T.* Vol.2, p.368.
21   Critchley *History of Police* pp.18-19.
22   *44th Account of... the Societies for Promoting Reformation of Manners,* referred to in Fryer *Mrs Grundy* p.292.
23   *Trial and Condemnation of... Earl of Castle-Haven* p.A3.
24   *The Women-Hater's Lamentation;* Dunton op. cit. No copy of the original 1707 edition of *He-Strumpets* has survived; Parks *John Dunton and the English Book Trade* p.348. The 1710 edition in *Athenianism* is described in its title as 'the fourth edition, altered and much enlarged'. Judging by the title, the additional material is that taken up with the sexual sins of women; this element appears as an afterthought to the initial homosexual passages. The molly house referred to in Ward op. cit. is probably the one, or one of those, broken up in 1707, although Ward is unclear as to whether he is describing a molly house which was still in existence when he was writing or one which had by then been broken up. The existence of the homosexual subculture is hinted at in the trial of Captain Rigby in 1698 (see note 38 below). There is the reference to St James's Park as the place where Rigby met Minton (see p.80 above). The author of the *Preface* to the *Tryal and Condemnation of... Earl of Castle-Haven* op. cit. p.A3 links the arrests in 1699 with 'the infamous example of that monster Ri... by, and other notorious sodomites', by which he probably means Rigby. Finally Rigby wanted to call to give evidence someone else who was at the tavern where the offence was supposed to have taken place, but was not allowed to do this as 'that gentleman stood indicted in the same indictment with him, for being aiding, advising, and assisting to him in committing his crime' (op. cit. p.241); the tavern may have been a molly house.
25   A raid on a molly house in 1725 is referred to on p.97 below.

26 Nor is there any sign of a more tolerant attitude. Unfortunately Professor Lawrence Stone's important and widely read book *Family, Sex and Marriage in England 1500-1800* is seriously adrift in his description of homosexuality in the eighteenth century, and of the molly houses in particular (pp.541-2). His view is that by the eighteenth century upper-class society in England had become more tolerant of homosexuality in comparison to the early part of the seventeenth century, while the hostility of the poor remained unchanged. As evidence of this he points to the greater number of men inheriting landed estates who remained unmarried; this may have been due, he suggests, to 'a rise in the number of homosexuals in this class'. The appearance of the molly houses, which he describes as 'homosexual clubs ... for the upper classes', are in his opinion further evidence of the same phenomenon. He contrasts this to the violence inflicted on sodomites in the pillory by the common people. The change in attitudes he explains as part of a general loosening of sexual restrictions in the period 1660-1770; he is also inclined to see it as a recurrent pattern: 'bisexual and homosexual instincts among men have usually been strongly condemned by the masses, but often tolerated by the elite' (pp.483-4). Apart from the unproblematic use of the term 'homosexuals', the most serious objection to this view is that the molly houses were not in any sense gentlemen's clubs. They cut across social classes with a bias rather towards the lower and lower-middle classes (see pp.85-6 above); the aristocracy were almost entirely absent (Trumbach op. cit., and a review of Professor Stone's book by Trumbach in *Journal of Social History* Vol.13, pp.136-43, where among other criticisms he points out the social ostracism homosexual behaviour could lead to in aristocratic circles). As to the large number of prosecutions for homosexual offences — which surely casts light on the views of the ruling classes — Professor Stone comments: 'But the fact that there were so many trials indicates that the forces of order still tried to punish those accused of this offence.' The 'forces of order' and the upper classes were not identical, but it is surely untenable to make this sharp distinction. However it has to be said that Professor Stone disarmingly admits that his work here is 'supported by [no] more than very fragmentary and inconclusive historical evidence' (p.616); and he is far from dogmatic.

27 *S.T.* Vol.2, p.362.

28 *S.T.* Vol.2, p.365.

29 *The Women-Hater's Lamentation.*

30 *S.T.* Vol.1, pp.105-8.

31 *S.T.* Vol.1, p.106.

32 *S.T.* Vol.2, p. 368.

33 *British Journal* 123, p.3, noted in Trumbach op. cit. p.22.
34 *S.T.* Vol.3, p.37.
35 *S.T.* Vol.3, pp.36-7.
36 *S.T.* Vol.2, p.363.
37 *S.T.* Vol.2, p.367.
38 *Compleat Collection of Remarkable Trials* Vol.1, pp.236-42. His extraordinarily vicious sentence (to stand three times in the pillory, a £1000 fine, a year in prison and to obtain sureties for seven years' good behaviour before his release) was probably a reaction to the 'blasphemy' involved (see *Tryal and Condemnation of... Earl of Castle-Haven*, Preface pp.A3 & A4, and *Calendar of State Papers, Domestic, 1698*, p.427). He made a fine show in the pillory, on the first occasion at least, probably having bribed the officials: 'Captain Rigby stood today upon the pillory, not with his head in it, dressed like a *beau;* so attended with constables and beadles that nobody could throw anything at him.' (*Calendar* op. cit. p.430.) His fine was partly commuted in December 1700 and an order for his release from prison was given in June 1701, that he might 'seek his fortune abroad' (*Calendar of State Papers, Domestic, 1 April 1700–8 March 1702* pp.80, 186, 322 and 357). One hopes that he succeeded.
39 *Compleat Collection of Remarkable Tryals* Vol.1, p.239. I have emended 'Forefather's' to 'forefathers''.
40 *Hell upon Earth* p.42.
41 *Annual Register 1763*, p.67 records a death in such circumstances, noted in Trumbach op. cit. p. 21.
41a British Museum *Political and Personal Satires* Vol.4 p.220. This is referred to in Stone *The Family, Sex and Marriage.*
42 Ward op. cit. p. 288.
43 *S.T.* Vol.2, p.370.
44 *S.T.* Vol.2, p.370.
45 *S.T.* Vol.2, p.362.
46 *S.T.* Vol.2, p.363.
47 Hooker *Works* Vol.1 p.237.
48 Locke *Essay* pp.618 and 410.
49 Quoted in Aaron *Theory of Universals* p.20.
50 Aaron op. cit. p.23.
51 Watt *Rise of the Novel.*
52 Ebeling *Modern Language Notes* Vol.52 pp.120-1, referred to in Watt op. cit.
53 Welleck *Rise of English Literary History* pp.14-44, referred to in Watt op. cit.
54 Freeman *English Emblem Books*, from whom this interpretation is taken.
55 Wither *Collection of Emblemes* pp.102 and 157; the same image, with a different significance, is used on p.74.

56 Hooker op. cit. Vol.1 pp.210 and 239.
57 Locke op. cit. p.299.
58 Butterfield *Origins of Modern Science* pp.191 ff.
59 Elliott *Old World and the New.*
60 Elliott op. cit. p.13.
61 McColley *Annals of Science* Vol.1, pp.385 ff.
62 McColley op. cit. p.398.
63 Quoted in McColley op. cit. p.423.
64 Trevor-Roper *Crisis in Europe* ed. Aston pp.59 ff.
65 Locke op. cit. p.695.
66 Thomas *Religion and the Decline of Magic* p.538.
67 Butterfield op. cit. p.174.
68 Stone *Family, Sex and Marriage* p.218.
69 Longmate *Workhouse* and Webb, S. and B. *English Local Government* Vol.7, part I, pp.101-313.
70 *Select Trials* Vol.3 pp.39-40.

Bibliography

This is not a reading list, but is intended rather as a note of the sources I have consulted and the editions I have used, with some indication for the non-specialist of their nature.

Manuscript Sources

Where the sources consulted in manuscript are included, in whole or in part, in calendars or other modern works this is acknowledged in the notes.

Bodleian
John Wilson: Ms. J. Walker/c. 2/460v

Greater London Record Office
Edward Bawde: MJ/SR/543/28-29, 202; MJ/SR/546/138; MJ/SR/554/109; MJ/SBR/1/579; MJ/SBR/2/236, 266, 351, 359
Alban Cooke: MJ/SR/519/121; MJ/SR/521/179; MJ/SR/537/217-219; MJ/SR/539/129-131; MJ/SR/546/66-69; MJ/CP/1/221
Peter de Guy: MJ/SR/562/63, 153, 169, 189; MJ/CP/2/137v
Richard Finch: MJ/SR/472/131; MJ/SBR/1/133; MJ/CP/1/69
George Willes: WJ/SR/12/128-129

Public Record Office
Domingo Cassedon Drago: Assizes/24/21 (69v) — (70)
Matthew Heaton: Assizes/35/22/9 m 40
James Slater: Assizes/35/49/4 mm 22, 44, 45, 67

Scottish Record Office
John Swan and John Litster: JC/1/13

Somerset Record Office
Meredith Davy: Q/SR/62
George Dowdeney: Q/SR/40

Sussex Record Office
John Wilson: QR/EW/57 (60) — (65)

Printed Sources

Trials, Legal Writings

Cockburn, J.S. (ed.) *Calendar of Assize Records: Essex, Hertfordshire, Kent, Surrey, Sussex Indictments Elizabeth I; Hertfordshire, Kent, Sussex Indictments James I* London, 1975-1980

Cockburn, J.S. (ed.) *Western Circuit Assize Orders 1629-1648, A Calendar* London, 1976

Coke, Edward *The Third Part of the Institutes of the Laws of England* London, 1644

Coke, Edward *The Twelfth Part of the Reports* London, 1656

Compleat Collection of Remarkable Tryals (anon.), Vol. 1, London, 1718

Emmison, F.G. *Elizabethan Life: Morals & the Church Courts. Mainly from Essex Archidiaconal Records* Chelmsford, 1973

Le Hardy, W. (ed.) *County of Middlesex Calendar to the Sessions Records* New Series, Vols 1-4, London, 1935-1941

Nicolas, H. (ed.) *Proceedings and Ordinances of the Privy Council of England* Vol. 7, London, 1837

Pitcairn, R. (ed.) *Criminal Trials in Scotland* Vol. 3, Edinburgh, 1833

Redwood, B.C. (ed.) *Quarter Sessions Order Book, 1642-1649* Sussex Record Society, Vol. 54, 1955

Select Trials for Murders, Robberies, Rapes, Sodomy, Coining, Frauds, and Other Offences at the Sessions-House in the Old Bailey (anon.), Vols 1-3, London, 1742

Whittaker, W.J. (ed.) *The Mirror of Justices* London, 1895

Social Satires

Brathwaite, Richard *Times Curtaine Drawne or the Anatomie of Vanitie* London, 1621

Breton, Nicholas *The Good and the Badde* in *The Works... of Nicholas Breton* (ed. A.B. Grosart), Vol. 2, Edinburgh, 1879

Butler, Samuel *Hudibras* (ed. J. Wilders), Oxford, 1967

Catalogue of Prints and Drawings in the British Museum: Division 1, Political and Personal Satires Vol. 4, 1883

C., R. *The Times' Whistle or a Newe Daunce of Seven Satires, and Other Poems* (ed. J.M. Cowper), London, 1871

Donne, John *John Donne. The Satires, Epigrams and Verse Letters* (ed. W. Milgate), Oxford, 1967

Drayton, Michael *The Moone-Calfe* in *The Works of Michael Drayton* (ed. W. Hebel), Vol. 3, Oxford, 1932, pp. 166 ff.

Dunton, John 'The He-Strumpets, a Satyr on the Sodomite Club' in *Athenianism* Vol. 2, London, 1710, pp. 93-99

Greene, Robert *Groats-worth of Witte, bought with a Million of Repentance* (ed. G.B. Harrison), Edinburgh, 1966

Guilpin, Edward *Skialetheia, or a Shadowe of Truth, in Certain Epigrams and Satyres* The Shakespeare Association Facsimiles, no. 2, Oxford and London, 1931

Hell upon Earth: or the Town in an Uproar (anon.), London, 1729

Jonson, Ben *On Sir Voluptvovs Beast* and *On the Same Beast* in *Ben Jonson* (ed. C.H. Herford and P. and E. Simpson), Vol. 8, Oxford, 1947

Marston, John *The Poems of John Marston* (ed. A. Davenport), Liverpool, 1961

Middleton, Richard *Epigrams and Satyres* (ed. J. Maidment), Edinburgh, 1840

Middleton, Thomas *The Black Book* in *The Works of Thomas Middleton* (ed. A.H. Bullen), Vol. 8, London, 1886, pp. 1-45

Middleton, Thomas, *Micro-Cynicon* in ibid., pp. 111-135

Nashe, Thomas *Pierce Penilesse His Supplication to the Diuell* in *The Works of Thomas Nashe* (ed. R.B. McKerrow), Vol. 1, Oxford, 1958

Satan's Harvest Home: or the Present State of Whorecraft, Adultery, Fornication, Procuring, Pimping, Sodomy, and the Game at Flatts (anon.), London, 1749

Stubbes, Philip *The Anatomie of Abuses* (ed. W.B.D.O. Turnbull), London and Edinburgh, 1836

Ward, Edward *The History of London Club[s]*, London, 1709

Other Poetry and Drama

Barnfield, Richard *The Complete Poems of Richard Barnfield* (ed. A.B. Grosart), London, 1876

Barnfield, Richard *Poems 1594-1598* (ed. E. Arber), Westminster, 1896

Drayton, Michael *Peirs Gaveston* in *The Works of Michael Drayton* Vol. 1, Oxford, 1931, pp. 157 ff.

Drummond William *Poetical Works of William Drummond of Hawthornden* (ed. L.E. Kastner), Edinburgh, 1913

Dryden, John *Dryden: The Dramatic Works* (ed. M. Summers), Vol. 1, London, 1931

Dunbar, William *The Poems of William Dunbar* (ed. J. Kingsley), Oxford, 1979

Fletcher, John *The Works of Francis Beaumont and John Fletcher* (ed. A.R. Waller), Cambridge, 1906

Jonson, Ben *Ben Jonson* (ed. C.H. Herford and P. Simpson), Vol. 4, Oxford, 1932

Marlowe, Christopher *The Complete Works of Christopher Marlowe* (ed. F. Bowers), Vol. 2, Cambridge, 1973

Milton, John *Poetical Works* (ed. D. Bush), Oxford, 1966

Shadwell, Thomas *The Complete Works of Thomas Shadwell* (ed. M. Summers), Vol. 5, London, 1927

Shakespeare, William *Shakespeare: Complete Works* (ed. W.J. Craig), Oxford, 1943

Sodom, or the Quintessence of Debauchery (ed.P.J. Kearney), typescript deposited in the British Library, 1969. On authorship, see note 74 to Chapter One.

Wilmot, John (Earl of Rochester) *Collected Works of John Wilmot, Earl of Rochester* (ed. J. Hayward), London, 1926

Wilmot, John (Earl of Rochester) *The Complete Poems of John Wilmot Earl of Rochester* (ed. D.M. Vieth), New Haven, 1968

Philosophy, Theology, History

Browne, Thomas *The Works of Sir Thomas Browne* (ed. G. Keynes), Vol. 2, London, 1928

Browne, Thomas *Religio Medici and Other Works* (ed. L.C. Martin), Oxford, 1964

Dante *The Divine Comedy of Dante Alighieri* (commentary by J.D. Sinclair) Vols 1 & 2, London, 1948

Holy Bible Authorised King James Version, 1611
Holy Bible Revised Standard Version, 1952
Hooker, Richard *The Works of... Richard Hooker* (arranged J. Keble, revised R.W. Church and F. Paget) Vol. 1, Oxford, 1888
James VI of Scotland (later James I of Great Britain and Ireland) Βασιλικὸν Δῶρον (Roxburghe Club edn), London, 1887
Lindsay, David *The Monarche* in *The Works of Sir David Lindsay* (ed. D. Hamer), Vol. 1, The Scottish Text Society, 1931, pp. 197-386
Locke, John *An Essay Concerning Human Understanding* (ed. P.H. Nidditch), Oxford, 1975
Raleigh, Walter *Sir Walter Raleigh's 'Sceptick'* in *The Works of Sir Walter Ralegh* (ed. T. Birch), Vol 2, London,1751, pp.331-340
Saluste du Bartas *The Divine Weeks and Works of Guillaume de Saluste Sieur du Bartas* (trans. Josua Sylvester, ed. S. Snyder), Oxford, 1979
Taylor, John *A Briefe Remembrance of all the English Monarchs, from the Norman Conquest, untill this Present* in *Works of John Taylor* Manchester, 1869
Wither, George *A Collection of Emblemes, Ancient and Moderne* (facsimile: intro. R. Freeman and notes C.S. Hensley), Columbia (S. Carolina), 1975

Biography, Personal Papers, Memoirs and Correspondence

Aubrey, John *Brief Lives* (ed. A. Clark), Oxford, 1898
Bradford, William *Bradford's History 'Of Plimouth Plantation'* (ed. Wright & Potter Printing Co.), Boston, 1898
Blencowe, R.W. *Paxhill and its Neighbourhood; with Extracts from the Manuscripts of the Wilson Family* Sussex Archaeological Collections Vol. 11, 1859, pp. 1-49
Danchin, F.C. 'Etudes Critiques sur Christopher Marlowe' in *Revue Germanique* Nov.-Dec. 1913, pp. 566-587. [Transcription of Harleian Mss. 6848 f. 487-9, 6853 f. 307-8, 6849 f. 218-9, 6848 f. 190-1, 7002 f. 10-11, 6849 f. 183 et. seq. concerning Christopher Marlowe and the circle of Walter Raleigh.]
D'Ewes, Simonds *The Autobiography and Correspondence of Sir Simonds D'Ewes* (ed. J.O. Halliwell), Vol. 1, London, 1845
Greg, W.W. (ed.) *English Literary Autographs, 1550-1650, Part I The Dramatists*, Oxford, 1925
Hutchinson, Lucy *Memoirs of the Life of Colonel Hutchinson* (ed.J. Hutchinson, revised C.H. Firth), London, 1906
Spedding, James *The Letters and the Life of Francis Bacon* Vol. 1, London, 1861
Walker, John *An Attempt towards Recovering an Account of the Numbers and Sufferings of the Clergy of the Church of England...*, London, 1714
Winthrop, John *The History of New England* (ed. J. Savage),Vol. 2, Boston, 1853
Wood, Anthony à *Athenae Oxonienses* (ed. P.Bliss), Vol. 2, London, 1815

Political and Religious Controversy, Broadsheets and Journalism

Annual Register for the Year 1763, The
Arraignment and Conviction of Mervin, Lord Audley Earl of Castlehaven, The (anon.), London, 1642
Bernard, Nicholas *The Penitent Death of a Woefull Sinner* London, 1642

Fish, Simon *A Supplication of the Poore Commons* in *A Supplicacyon for the Beggers etc.* (ed. J.M. Cowper), London,1871

British Journal, The no. 123, 23 January 1725

Life and Death of John Atherton Lord Bishop of Waterford and Lysmore, The (anon.), London, 1641

London Journal, The 4 August 1722

Of the Horrible and Wofull Destruction of, Sodome and Gomorra. To the Tune of the Nine Muses (anon.), London, n.d.

Osborne, Francis (attributed to) *Traditionall Memoyres on the Raigne of King Iames,* 1658

Pagitt, Ephraim *Heresiography* London, 1647

Persecutio Undecima (anon.), London, 1648

Peyton, Edward *The Divine Catastrophe of the Kingly Family of the House of Stuarts* in *Secret History of the Court of James I* Vol. 2, Edinburgh, 1811, pp. 301-466

Rainolds, John *Th'Overthrow of Stage-Playes* 1599

Sodom Fair: or, the Market of the Man of Sin (anon.), 1658

Tryal and Condemnation of Mervin, Lord Audley Earl of Castle-Haven, The (anon.), 1699

Walker, Clement *Relations and Observations . . . upon the Parliament begun Anno Dom. 1640. Book 2: Anarchia Anglicana: or the History of Independency* London, 1661

Weldon, Anthony *The Court and Character of King James* London, 1651

White, John *The First Century of Scandalous, Malignant Priests* London, 1643

Women-Hater's Lamentation, The (anon.), London, 1707

Administrative

Ainsworth, J. (ed.) *Prerogative Court of Canterbury Administrations* Vol. 1 (1649-1654), The British Record Society, The Index Library, 1944

Arber, E. (ed.) *A Transcript of the Registers of the Company of Stationers of London 1554-1640* Vol. 3, London, 1876

Attree, F.W.T.(ed.) *Notes of Post Mortem Inquisitions taken in Sussex. 1 Henry VII to 1649 and after* Lewes, 1912

Bateson, E. (ed.) *Calendar of State Papers, Domestic Series, Of the Reign of William III. 1 Jan.- 31 Dec. 1698* London, 1933

Bateson, E. (ed.) *Calendar of State Papers, Domestic Series, Of the Reign of William III 1 April 1700 - 8 March 1702* London, 1937

Dunkin, E.H.W. (ed. D. MacLeod) *Calendar of Sussex Marriage Licences* Sussex Record Society, Vol. 12, Lewes, 1911

Journals of the House of Commons Vol. 3, 1803

Sawyer, F.E. *Proceedings of the Committee of Plundered Ministers Relating to Sussex* Sussex Archaeological Collections, Vol. 36, 1888, pp. 136-159

Descriptions by Travellers

Herbert, Thomas *A Discription of the Persian Monarchy . . . A Relation of Some Yeares Travaile* London, 1634

Lithgow, William, *The Totall Discourse of the Rare Adventures and Painful Peregrinations of Long Nineteene Yeares Travayles* (ed. James Maclehose & Co.), Glasgow, 1906

Turbervile, George *The Author being in Moscouia* in *Tragical Tales, and Other Poems* Edinburgh, 1837, pp.370 ff.

Dictionaries and Maps

Florio, John *Queen Anna's New World of Words* London, 1611
Huloet, Richard *Abcedarium Anglico-Latinum* London, 1552
Rocque, John *A Plan of the Cities of London and Westminster and Borough of Southwark* (ed. H. Margary, with introductory notes by J. Howgego), Lympne Castle and Chichester, 1971

Secondary Works

Aaron, R.I. *The Theory of Universals* Oxford, 1967
Aston, T. (ed.) *Crisis in Europe, 1560-1660* London, 1965
Bailey, D.S. *Homosexuality and the Western Christian Tradition* London, 1955
Baine, R.M. 'Rochester or Fishbourne: a Question of Authorship' in *Review of English Studies* Vol. 22, no. 87, pp. 201 ff. (July 1946)
Baker, J.H. (ed.) *Legal Records & the Historian* London, 1978
Bingham, C. 'Seventeenth-Century Attitudes towards Deviant Sex' in *The Journal of Interdisciplinary History* Vol. 1, no. 3, pp. 447-468 (Spring 1971)
Bingham, C. *James I of England* London, 1981
Boas, F.S. *Christopher Marlowe: a Biographical and Critical Study* Oxford, 1940
Boas, F.S. 'Informer Against Marlowe' in *Times Literary Supplement* Vol. 48, p. 608 (16 Sept 1949)
Boon, L.J. 'Those Damned Sodomites: Public Images of Sodomy in the Eighteenth-Century Netherlands' in K. Gerard and G. Hekma (eds.) *The Pursuit of Sodomy: Male Homosexuality in Renaissance and Enlightenment Europe* New York, 1989, pp. 237-48; *Journal of Homosexuality* Vol. 16, nos 1/2 (1988)
Bossy, J. 'The Character of Elizabethan Catholicism' in T. Aston (ed.) *Crisis in Europe* loc. cit., pp. 223-246
Boswell, J. *Christianity, Social Tolerance and Homosexuality. Gay People in Western Europe from the Beginning of the Christian Era to the Fourteenth Century* Chicago and London, 1980
Braudel, F. *Capitalism and Material Life 1400-1800* London, 1973
Bray, A. 'Homosexuality and the Signs of Male Friendship in Elizabethan England' in *History Workshop* Issue 29, pp. 1-19 (Spring 1990); reprinted with minor alterations in J. Goldberg (ed.) *Queering the Renaissance* Durham and London, 1994, pp. 40-61
Bredbeck, G.W. *Sodomy and Interpretation: Marlowe to Milton* Ithaca and London, 1991
Bullough, V. Le R. *Sex, Society, & History* New York, 1976
Bullough, V. Le R. *Sexual Variance in Society and History* New York, 1976
Butterfield, H. *The Origins of Modern Society* London, 1949
Carpenter, E. *The Intermediate Sex. A Study of Some Transitional Types of Men and Women* London, 1916
Carrasco, R. *Inquisición y represión sexual en Valencia: Historia de los sodomitas (1565-1785)* Barcelona, 1985
Chancellor, E.B. *The Pleasure Haunts of London during Four Centuries* London, 1925

Cockburn, J.S. 'The Nature and Incidence of Crime in England 1559-1625: a Preliminary Survey' in J.S. Cockburn (ed.) *Crime in England 1550-1880* London, 1977, pp. 49-71

Cockburn, J.S. 'Trial by the Book? Fact and Theory in the Criminal Process 1558-1628' in J.H. Baker (ed.) *Legal Records and the Historian* op. cit, pp. 60 ff.

Cockburn, J.S. 'Early-Modern Assize Records as Historical Evidence' in *Journal of the Society of Archivists* Vol. 5, no. 4, pp. 215-231 (October 1975)

Critchley, T.A. *A History of Police in England and Wales 900-1966*, London, 1967

Crompton, L. 'Homosexuals and the Death Penalty in Colonial America' in *Journal of Homosexuality* Vol. 1, pp. 277-294 (Spring 1976)

Ebeling, H.L. 'The Word *Anachronism*' in *Modern Language Notes* Vol. 52, no. 2, pp. 120-121 (Feb. 1937)

Eccles, M. 'Marlowe in Newgate' in *Times Literary Supplement* Vol. 33, p. 604 (6 Sept. 1934)

Eccles, M. 'Marlowe in Kentish Tradition' in *Notes & Queries,* Vol. 169, pp. 20-23, 39-41, 58-61 and 'Marlowe in Kentish Tradition: a Supplementary Note', ibid., pp. 134-35 (July-Dec. 1935)

Elliott, J.H. *The Old World and the New 1492-1650* Cambridge, 1970

Ellis, H. *Studies in the Psychology of Sex. Part Four: Sexual Inversion* London, 1942

Flandrin, J.L. *Families in Former Times: Kinship, Household and Sexuality* Cambridge, 1979

Foucault, M. *The History of Sexuality. Volume 1: an Introduction* London, 1979

Freeman, R. *English Emblem Books* London, 1948

Fryer, P. *Mrs Grundy: Studies in English Prudery* London, 1963

Garde, N.I. (pseud. for E. Leoni) *Jonathan to Gide. The Homosexual in History* New York, 1964

Goldberg, J. 'Sodomy and Society: The Case of Christopher Marlowe' in *Southwest Review* Vol. 69, no. 4, pp. 371-378, (Autumn 1984). A slightly revised version appeared in David Scott Kastan and Peter Stallybrass (eds.) *Staging the Renaissance* New York, 1991, pp. 75-82

Goldberg, J. *Sodometries: Renaissance Texts, Modern Sexualities* Stanford, 1992

Goodich, M. *The Unmentionable Vice: Homosexuality in the Later Medieval Period* Santa Barbara and Oxford, 1979

Hajnal, J. 'European Marriage Patterns in Perspective' in *Population in History: Essays in Historical Demography* (ed. D.V. Glass and D.E.C. Eversley), London, 1965, pp. 101 ff.

Harris, W. (ed.) *Sir James Ware's History of the Bishops of the Kingdom of Ireland* Dublin, 1739

Hill, C. *The World Turned Upside Down: Radical Ideas during the English Revolution* Harmondsworth, 1975

Hill, C. 'Male Homosexuality in 17th-Century England' in *The Collected Essays of Christopher Hill, Volume 3: People and Ideas in 17th-Century England* Brighton, 1986, pp. 226-35

Hook, L. 'Something More about Rochester' in *Modern Language Notes* Vol. 75, pp. 478-485 (June 1960)

Karlen, A. *Sexuality and Homosexuality* London, 1971

Katz, J. *Gay American History: Lesbians and Gay Men in the U.S.A.* New York, 1976

Kernan, A. *The Cankered Muse: Satire of the English Renaissance* New Haven, 1959

Laslett, T.P. *The World We Have Lost* London, 1965

Laslett, T.P. 'The Wrong Way Through the Telescope: a Note on Literary Evidence in Sociology and in Historical Sociology' in *British Journal of Sociology* Vol. 27, no. 3, pp. 319-42 (Sept. 1976)

Laslett, T.P. *Family Life and Illicit Love in Earlier Generations: Essays in Historical Sociology* Cambridge, 1977

Laslett, T.P. (ed. and intro.) with the assistance of R. Wall *Household and Family in Past Time* Cambridge, 1972

Lehman, J. *Holborn: An Historical Portrait of a London Borough* London, 1970

Lemert, E.M. *Human Deviance, Social Problems, and Social Control* New Jersey, 1967

Longmate, N. *The Workhouse* London, 1974

Macfarlane, A.D.J. *The Regulation of Marital and Sexual Relations in Seventeenth Century England, with Special Reference to the County of Essex* University of London M. Phil. thesis, 1968

Macfarlane, A. *Witchcraft in Tudor and Stuart England* London, 1970

Marshall, J. 'Pansies, Perverts and Macho Men: Changing Conceptions of Male Homosexuality' in K. Plummer (ed.) *The Making of the Modern Homosexual* loc. cit., pp. 133-154

Matthews, A.G. *Walker Revised* Oxford, 1948

McColley, G. 'The Seventeenth-Century Doctrine of a Plurality of Worlds' *Annals of Science* Vol. 1, pp. 385-430 (Oct. 1936)

McIntosh, M. 'The Homosexual Role' in *Social Problems* Vol. 16, no. 2, pp. 182-192 (1968); reprinted in K. Plummer (ed.) *The Making of the Modern Homosexual* loc. cit., pp. 30-44 with 'Postscript: "The Homosexual Role" Revisited', pp. 44-49

Monter, E.W. 'la Sodimie à l'Époque Moderne en Suisse Romande' in *Annales Économies Sociétés Civilisations* Vol. 29, pp. 1023-33 (1974)

Morgan, E.S. 'The Puritans & Sex' in *New England Quarterly* Vol. 15, pp. 591-607 (December 1942)

Mott, L. 'Portuguese Pleasures: The Gay Subculture in Portugal at the Time of the Inquisition' in *Homosexuality, Which Homosexuality?* Papers of the International Scientific Conference on Gay and Lesbian Studies, December 15-18, 1987, London and Amsterdam, pp. 85-95

Oaks, R.F. ' "Things Fearful to Name": Sodomy and Buggery in Seventeenth-Century New England' in *Journal of Social History* Vol. 12, no. 2, pp. 268-81 (Winter 1978-79)

Oxford English Dictionary, The Vols 3, 6, 10, Oxford, 1933

Parks, S. *John Dunton and the English Book Trade* New York and London, 1976

Peter, J. *Complaint and Satire in Early English Literature* Oxford, 1956

Plummer, K. *Sexual Stigma: an Interactionist Account* London, 1975

Plummer, K. 'Building a Sociology of Homosexuality' in K. Plummer (ed.) *The Making of the Modern Homosexual* loc. cit., pp. 17-29

Plummer, K. (ed.) *The Making of the Modern Homosexual* London, 1981

Quaife, G.R. 'The Consenting Spinster in a Peasant Society: Aspects of Premarital Sex in "Puritan" Somerset 1645-1660' in *Journal of Social History* Vol. 11, no. 2, pp. 228-44 (Winter 1977-78)

Quaife, G.R. *Wanton Wenches and Wayward Wives: Peasants and Illicit Sex In Early Seventeenth Century England* London, 1979

Rey, M. 'Parisian Homosexuals Create a Lifestyle, 1700-1750: The Police Archives' in Robert P. Maccubbin (ed.) *Unauthorized Sexual Behavior during the Enlightenment* College of William and Mary, 1985, pp. 179-91, Special Issue of *Eighteenth-Century Life* Vol. 9, n.s., 3 (May 1985)

Rey, M. 'Police and Sodomy in Eighteenth-Century Paris: From Sin to Disorder' in K. Gerard and G. Hekma (eds.) *The Pursuit of Sodomy: Male Homosexuality in Renaissance and Enlightenment Europe* New York, 1989, pp. 129-46, *Journal of Homosexuality* Vol. 16, nos 1/2 (1988). See the author's Memoire de Maitrise defended at the University of Paris, partly published in French in 'Police et Sodomie a Paris au XVIIIᵉ Siècle: Du Péché au Désordre' *Revue d'histoire moderne et contemporaine* Vol. 29, pp. 113-24 (1982)

Rowse, A.L. *Homosexuals in History: A Study of Ambivalence in Society, Literature and the Arts* London, 1977

Russell, J.B. *Witchcraft in the Middle Ages* Ithaca and London, 1972

Ruggiero, G. 'Sexual Criminality in the Early Renaissance. Venice 1338-58' in *Journal of Social History* Vol. 8, no. 4, pp. 18-37 (Summer 1974-75)

Ruggiero, G. *The Boundaries of Eros: Sex Crime and Sexuality in Renaissance Venice* New York, 1985. Review by Alan Bray in K. Gerard and G. Hekma (eds.) *The Pursuit of Sodomy: Male Homosexuality in Renaissance and Enlightenment Europe* New York, 1989, pp. 499-505, *Journal of Homosexuality* Vol. 16, nos 1/2 (1988)

Sedgwick, E.K. *Between Men: English Literature and Male Homosocial Desire* New York, 1985

Smith, B.R. *Homosexual Desire in Shakespeare's England: A Cultural Poetics* Chicago and London, 1991

Smith, S.R. 'The London Apprentices as Seventeenth-Century Adolescents' in *Past and Present* Vol. 61, pp. 149 ff. (November 1973)

Stone, L. *The Family, Sex and Marriage in England, 1500-1800* London, 1977; all references are to this edition unless otherwise stated

Stone, L. *The Family, Sex and Marriage in England, 1500-1800* (Pelican edn), Harmondsworth, 1979

Steakley, J.D. 'Sodomy in Enlightenment Prussia: From Execution to Suicide' in K. Gerard and G. Hekma (eds.) *The Pursuit of Sodomy: Male Homosexuality in Renaissance and Enlightenment Europe* New York, 1989, pp. 163-75; *Journal of Homosexuality* Vol. 16, nos 1/2 (1988)

Stephen, L. (ed.) *Dictionary of National Biography* Vol. 2, London, 1885

Tatham, G.B. *Dr John Walker and the Sufferings of the Clery* Cambridge, 1911

Taylor, G.R. *Sex in History* London, 1953

Thomas, K. *Religion and the Decline of Magic* Harmondsworth, 1973

Tillyard, E.M. *The Elizabethan World Picture,* London, 1967

Trevor-Roper, H.R. 'The General Crisis of the Seventeenth Century' (with related articles) in T. Aston (ed.) *Crisis in Europe* loc. cit. pp. 59 ff.

Trevor-Roper, H.R. 'The European Witch-Craze of the Sixteenth and Seventeenth Centuries' in *Religion, the Reformation and Social Change and Other Essays* London, 1967, pp. 90-192

Trumbach, R. 'London's Sodomites: Homosexual Behaviour and Western Culture in the 18th Century' in *Journal of Social History* Vol. 11, no. 1, pp. 1-33 (Fall 1977-78)

Trumbach, R. 'Europe and its Families: A Review Essay of Lawrence Stone, *The Family, Sex and Marriage in England 1500-1800*' in *Journal of Social History* Vol. 13, no. 1, pp. 136-43 (Fall 1979-80)

Trumbach, R. 'Gender and the Homosexual Role in Modern Western Culture: The 18th and 19th Centuries Compared' in Dennis Altman and others (eds.) *Homosexuality, Which Homosexuality? International Conference on Gay and Lesbian Studies,* London and Amsterdam, 1989, pp. 149-69

Trumbach, R. 'The Birth of the Queen: Sodomy and the Emergence of Gender Equality in Modern Culture, 1660-1750' in M.B. Duberman, M. Vicinus, and G. Chauncey (eds.) *Hidden from History: Reclaiming the Gay and Lesbian Past* New York and Ontario, 1989, pp. 129-40

Trumbach, R. 'London's Sapphists: From Three Sexes to Four Genders in the Making of Modern Culture' in G. Herdt (ed.) *Third Sex, Third Gender: Beyond Sexual Dimorphism in Culture and History* New York, 1994, pp. 111-36

Van der Meer, T. 'The Persecutions of Sodomites in Eighteenth-Century Amsterdam: Changing Perceptions of Sodomy' in K. Gerard and G. Hekma (eds.) *The Pursuit of Sodomy: Male Homosexuality in Renaissance and Enlightenment Europe* New York, 1989, pp. 263-307; *Journal of Homosexuality* Vol. 16, nos 1/2 (1988). This is mainly an extensive summary of the author's study *De wesentljke sonde van sodomie en andere vuyligheenden: Sodomietenvervolgingen in Amsterdam 1730-1811* Amsterdam 1984

Van der Meer, T. 'Sodomy and the Pursuit of a Third Sex in the Early Modern Period' in G. Herdt (ed.) *Third Sex, Third Gender: Beyond Sexual Dimorphism in Culture and History* New York, 1994, pp. 137-212

Vieth, D.M. *Attribution in Restoration Poetry* New Haven and London, 1963

Ward, H.G. 'Joachim Du Bellay and Sir Thomas Browne' in *Review of English Studies* Vol. 5, pp. 59-60 (January 1929)

Watt, I.P. *The Rise of the Novel: Studies in Defoe, Richardson and Fielding* London, 1957

Webb, S. and B. *English Local Government Vol. 7: English Poor Law History* London, 1927

Weeks, J. ' "Sins and Disease": Some Notes on Homosexuality in the Nineteenth Century' in *History Workshop* Vol. 1, pp. 211-19 (Spring 1976)

Weeks, J. *Coming Out: Homosexual Politics in Britain from the Nineteenth Century to the Present* London, 1977

Weeks, J. 'Movements of Affirmation: Sexual Meanings and Homosexual Identities in *Radical History Review* Vol. 20, pp. 164-79 (Spring-Summer 1979)

Weeks, J. 'Capitalism and the Organisation of Sex' in Gay Left Collective (ed.) *Homosexuality: Power & Politics* London, 1980

Weeks, J. 'Discourse, Desire and Sexual Deviance: Some Problems in a History of Homosexuality' in K. Plummer (ed.) *The Making of the Modern Homosexual* loc. cit., pp. 76-111

Weeks, J. *Sex, Politics and Society: the Regulation of Sexuality Since 1800* London, 1981

Welleck, R. *The Rise of English Literary History* New York, 1966

Wheatley, H.B. *London Past and Present. Its History, Associations and Traditions* Vol. 1, London, 1891

Zagorin, P. *The Court and the Country: the Beginning of the English Revolution* London, 1969

Index

By Peter Daniels

Between Men ~ Between Women

Lesbian and Gay Studies

Lillian Faderman and Larry Gross, Editors